JACK LLEWELLYN SYSTEM

D0168607

Get the Mud Out of the Water

MAKE LIFE-CHANGING DECISIONS

Dr. Jack Llewellyn, Ph.D.

SERVING PUBLISHERS & AUTHORS
PA SERVICES

To my beautiful, caring children—Hunter, Tripp, Tate, and Abbott.

I needed a lot of help with this project. Thanks go to Joe Pruss, Burtch Hunter, and Donna Miller for delivering on short notice.

SERVING PUBLISHERS & AUTHORS
PASERVICES

Published by
PA Services, LLC
4716 Buckskin Trail
Lilburn, Georgia 30047

Copyright 2012 by Dr. Jack H. Llewellyn, Ph.D.

ISBN 978-0-9844652-2-4

Printed in the United States of America

Author photo by Tripp Llewellyn

Cover and book design by Burtch Hunter Design

Get the Mud Out of the Water

As a professional athlete, I'm always looking for an edge—especially a mental edge—and Jack Llewellyn's program has helped me greatly in that area. Jack's program has helped me deal with adversity, make the necessary adjustments, and recover. Jack has been a huge help with the mental side of my game.

Tom Glavine

NL Cy Young Award Winner, 1991 and 1998, future Hall of Famer

Jack Llewellyn is a master at telling memorable stories that illustrate life lessons. His advice is extremely valuable because it can be applied in corporate settings as well as in one's personal life. I utilize the techniques I have learned from him every day to help me achieve.

Greg Poplarski

Senior Vice President, Allianz Global Investors

Whether it be the importance of teamwork, overcoming adversity, receiving excellent coaching, or the merits of practice, savvy business managers have long illustrated their points through analogies to sports. Jack Llewellyn has an uncanny way of showing how winning in sports translates to the broader arena of winning in business.

Lonnie Cooper

Chairman and CEO, Career Sports Entertainment, Inc.

I met Jack in 1992 when I had just been traded from the Cincinnati Reds to the New York Yankees. It is no coincidence my best years in baseball were in New York. Thank you, Jack, for helping me change my career and realizing how my faith could drive me on and off the field.

Paul O'Neill

Former All-Star outfielder and American League Batting Champion for the New York Yankees

Jack Llewellyn's approach is simple and straightforward, and it can be applied to all areas of the professional workplace as well as to everyday life. Jack's program teaches you how to adapt to and overcome pressure and increases your ability to persevere and get better, instead of giving in and getting frustrated. Jack has helped me tremendously."

John Smoltz

NL Cy Young Award Winner, 1996, future Hall of Famer

I was privileged to have known and worked with Jack Llewellyn for over sixteen years. His help was directly related to the Atlanta Braves' great success.

Bobby Cox

Future Hall of Fame manager, Atlanta Braves

PREFACE

I've spent many years talking with athletes, corporate executives, salespeople and people with chronic illnesses, especially those folks with multiple sclerosis, about the importance of being able to recover quickly from adversity. This book is the result of those experiences and offers you a very practical, workable, step-by-step program for quick recovery.

Since quicker recovery from adversity seems to be a dry, boring title, I talked with Joe Pruss, as the only person who has heard me speak on several occasions with this diverse group of folks. My question was, "What do I say when I talk about recovery techniques?" Joe's response was, "You always talk about getting the mud out of the water; being able to clear your mind. After much thought and analysis of the factors which enable me to recover from significant adversity, his comment made perfect sense. Before you can recover, you must clear your mind as much as possible to be able to categorize and prioritize the remaining mind-clutter, the remaining mud. Thus the title of this book, *Get the Mud Out of the Water.*

This book offers easy to learn, practical tools which can be applied in every situation. During a self-evaluation, you will discover that your assets far outweigh your liabilities. Your assets, when used properly, will give you a higher self-image and a higher level of self-confidence. Several interviews with participants that have had significant adversities are included in this book. These real accounts of people recovering from adversity prove the system works. You will also realize that your energy level will be higher, and that you can use that renewed energy in a more efficient and a more effective manner. This is the ultimate guide for anyone who is dealing with adversity. Beginning with the first chapter, you will be able to recognize mind clutter. In the following chapters you will begin to recognize assets, many of which are taken for granted or not previously recognized. Stress will become an incentive to succeed instead of a detriment to you, both personally and professionally. There is no requirement for being able to challenge daily stressors. Being tired and lethargic will be much less a detriment to functioning in your daily life. Moments of depression will decrease and conversations regarding your adversity will become easier, more open and honest.

Personally, I have experienced periods of significant adversity. These times have had a negative impact on me professionally, financially and socially. It wasn't until I began to personally live the program I had been teaching over the past three decades to world-class athletes, corporate executives and people with chronic illnesses, that I changed my life. I've become the person I've wanted to be and should have been for a very long time. The most significant lesson I've learned is that the better care you take of yourself, the more positive energy you have for others. My performance enhancement program, which has been internationally acclaimed, has become significantly more effective through my own experiences with adversity.

The pre-requisite for using the system is a willingness to honestly determine where you are in your life. You need to decide where you want to be in the future—starting today. You must recognize that winners in life don't only personally win or only professionally win. Winners win both personally and professionally. It's virtually impossible to have only one side of your life in order and be a success. For example, in golf, you cannot have order in your game, unless you have order before every shot. Hence, the pre-shot routine. Another example deals with the popular concept of "multitasking." Too often there is so much emphasis on multitasking that you learn to do several things at an average level and nothing really well. I tell MS patients, for example, do one thing at a time and do it well. This is where self-evaluation becomes so critical. If you use too much energy trying to do several things, then you don't have enough energy to recover from adversity which might occur in any number of your several tasks. You will learn how to allocate your energy with those you want to involve on your team. You will learn how to place yourself in an environment conducive to recovery, and perhaps more importantly, how to recognize when you have recovered. Armed with a feeling of personal power not previously felt, you will be able to face and even look forward to adversity with renewed self-confidence.

The challenge is simple. Make a decision regarding your life. Where are you today and where do you want to be tomorrow? Armed with this self-knowledge, you can then proceed with this book to help you get there. Read it, use it and move to a much higher level psychologically, which will enable you to approach every day with positive expectations. Realizing that positive outcomes can come from the darkest days is an incredible and empowering feeling.

CHAPTER 1

Define and Recognize the Mud in the Water

This is the beginning of a life changing experience. Enjoy this conversation I am having with you. Learn to get the most you can from every day for the rest of your life by learning how to deal with the mud in the water. Loosely defined, mud in the water consists of thoughts, ideas, concerns, and anything else that is in your thought processing system. The mud gets there through receptors in your neurological system which constantly receives information. This information may or may not be important to execute the task at hand. In fact, much of this extraneous information only interferes with your focus and your concentration. For example, information that is uncontrollable by you is fed into your system causing worry resulting in wasted energy. Consequently, you don't have enough energy left to devote to your intended task. It is common knowledge that most of our energy is spent on thinking about uncontrollables. Individually, you must be able to recognize your mud, to list the things you consider to be both positive and negative that you think about on a daily basis. Not all mud is negative. It's clutter, including things you don't want to forget, but may not need to think about all the time. As an example, my father, who loved what I did during my career, didn't necessarily understand what I did, but nevertheless, he loved it. He died 29 years ago. But during those last few months when he had cancer and was paralyzed, I was able to sit with him in the hospital and watch baseball games and just say nothing, but it was an experience that I'll never forget. I remember it to this day and I think about him every single day. But there are times, when I'm speaking at meetings or doing seminars, working with athletes that I need to be focused and don't really have time to sit and think about our good times. And I don't want this to sound like a cold, uncaring statement, but I compartmentalize thoughts of him. I put him in a drawer in my brain so that when I have time later, I can open that drawer and take him out and think about him as long as I want. You see, mud in the water is very personal, it's yours. It's not to be considered the business of anybody else, except those people you trust and people you have on your team and those special people you can talk with any time, day or night. Your mind will never be clear, but you can prioritize your thoughts. There are three personal categories of mind clutter.

1. Things you want to act on and need to act on for task execution.

2. Things you need to eliminate, perhaps with the help of your team members.

3. The things you need to put in a "mental drawer" as I do with my dad until you can devote mental time for them.

Everybody has all three categories of clutter in their mind. Some people obviously more than others. Those people who would tell you that they have peace of mind are people who have learned to deal with the mud in the water. They've learned to categorize or, as many people would say, compartmentalize. They've learned to focus; they've learned that when they are receiving information they can eliminate some of that information before it gets to the through processing center. I've been blessed over my career to work with the greatest athletes in the world, some top corporate executives and to work with young athletes and probably most rewarding to work with MS patients over the last seven years. I have spent almost 40 years trying to help athletes and corporate employees get the mud out of the water, helping them to clear their minds as much as possible in order to recover more quickly from adversity. I've probably received more emotional satisfaction over the last seven years than the previous 33 years. Why? Simply because the things that I've been able to do and the people that I've been able to touch emotionally are the most grateful people, the most appreciative people that I have ever known. After I was diagnosed with MS, I was privileged to start a journey with patients that has continued around the U.S. I never realized that I was going to be able to influence people's lives or at the very least to cause people to think about their lives and realize what they had to offer not only to themselves but to other people. Even though many of them have physical disabilities, some have mental dysfunctions, others have cognitive issues, but they always seem to appreciate the honesty that I bring to the meetings and the challenges that I bring to the meetings to help them learn to help themselves. Based on my experiences with those folks over the last few years, I promised myself that my next book would be dedicated to helping people to mentally recover quicker from adversity. I want you to understand that everybody has limitations, but everyone can use their assets to achieve personal fulfillment. To be able to open a new world to people emotionally is very special. I also am committed to talking with you. I want you to read this book feeling like you and I are having a good old fashioned conversation. It's not a complicated literary masterpiece by any stretch of the imagination. It's simply meant to cause you to think about your life, to realize that you are a special person with tremendous emotionally potential.

The first step is to spend time thinking about the mud in your water. What do you think about daily? What are some things you wish did not take up space in your mind? When you're trying to focus on a task, what interferes with that focus? It's no one's business to evaluate your emotional trauma, to evaluate which things are important or not important to you, to evaluate which things you want to compartmentalize and what things you have to learn to live with. It's your responsibility. It's your decision to make. In your lifetime, there are no immunities to adversity. Everyone at every age has adversity. You need to develop a plan to store in your mental bank to deal with adversity more quickly with positive, rewarding results. Some people recover quickly, some let adversity dictate the recovery time. Some people recover to win. Some recover only to survive. Some quit and some lose self confidence and even their lives. Some people who I consider to be the winners are people who seek out success every day. The people who thrive on stress, the people who see adversity as a challenge seek out adversity to satisfy a thirst for challenge and risk taking. Some people use adversity as a cover for fear of success or fear of failure. Every person must make a decision every time adversity rears its ugly head. At least if you have the appropriate tools in your bag, you will be equipped to make a decision, to set a course of action and to execute to recovery. Recovery is not magic and it's not automatic. Many times time sis not your friend when it comes to recovery. The most successful people are those who speed the process of recovery. Sometimes we have to be realistic and settle for a certain degree of recovery, which is okay if you keep your focus and you are able to go back to it later and complete the task. Certain adversities are a part of life, and we must learn to live with those. It's not for me to say here, that you can do anything that you want to do and that life's a bed of roses and that if you can see it you can do it. Those things are not true in real life. In real life you are going to have challenges every day. In real life, as you get older or as you become disabled, as you have cognitive issues, you find that you can't recover as quickly, and that's okay, but you can recover. It's interesting that when you mention recovering from adversity, the word recovery many times has a negative connotation. It's almost like in my profession of sports psychology, the word psychology carries a negative connotation. Through trial and error over the years, I learned to rename my program and call it mental development or mental coaching and then all of a sudden everyone wants to participate. What I want you to do throughout the rest of the book is to read and think about each chapter to enable you to (1) List the mud in the water in no priority order. Then you'll be asked to evaluate your assets and liability, to pick team members who will either supplement your assets or take away your liabilities. For example, if I'm sitting in a corporate meeting with five people they're all on my team and I have five assets and five liabilities and I put them on the table. If each person at the table has an asset to offset one of my liabilities, I can get up and walk away with ten assets and when I get in trouble in a meeting or trouble in execution of a task, I can call my team members. You see, we need to share this information with those who are important, those who are closest to us. Once you have your team in place, then you're able to understand the process of motivation a little better. Recognize the incentives, the things that drive you to do what you do. And you're able to have a better understanding of how much more important it is to be intrinsically motivated as opposed to extrinsically motivated. You learn how important the environment is to success. I've always felt that the environment and the people in that environment enable you to be successful or can actually cause you to be unsuccessful. Many times, just a change in environment is healthy. I've seen athletes on baseball teams not play well, not hit well, be traded to another team in another city and play, hit and perform at a very high level—the coach is not better, the management is not better, it's just the change in environment that's beneficial to those people. It's not just in sports, you see it in corporate offices where people work in an environment that may not be conducive to their assets and attention is called to their liabilities on a daily basis. So they become survivors and try to not fail and try to not lose. You put those same people in a positive environment with positive reinforcement and those people become star performers. Now everybody needs to be made aware of things that are not going well, but for every one thing that you recognize in a person that's not going well, you need to finish that conversation by recognizing things that they do well so that they listen and they walk away feeling better about themselves and they're more motivated to correct the faults that they might have. It's very important that at the end of this first chapter that you take the time and you recognize and you list those things that you consider to be clutter in your mind. And then that you categorize those things as is suggested on the worksheets. After you do that, the rest of the book is meant to help you to deal with the mud in the water. Now have fun, enjoy the book and when you read it, I'd like you to feel like it's not necessarily an academic, education endeavor, but rather a conversation that from 40 years experience I think will help you to think about your life and make changes where they are needed.

MUD IN THE WATER

(THINGS ON YOUR MIND, BOTH + AND −)

1. _____

2. _____

3. _____

4. _____

5. _____

6. _____

7. _____

8. _____

9. _____

10. _____

MUD TO COMPARTMENTALIZE

1. _____

2. _____

3. _____

4. _____

5. _____

MUD TO ELIMINATE

1. _____

2. _____

3. _____

4. _____

5. _____

MUD YOU MUST LIVE WITH

1. _____

2. _____

3. _____

4. _____

5. _____

CHAPTER 2

Build a Strong Foundation Around Your Assets

If you've ever read any of my books, you'll always find a chapter dealing with assets and liabilities. I think it's the foundation for success, an understanding of those assets and liabilities. It also seems that when people are having adversity or have too much mud in the water, that they spend most of their time avoiding their liabilities and very little time flaunting their assets; assets being those things that make you good at what you do and make you who you are. The liabilities are those things that drive people nuts. Liabilities are the things that you need to do, but perhaps don't do well. Those things that you can't control, for the most part, seem to be liabilities. And so when we begin to worry or use emotional energy, we usually expend more of that energy on avoiding our liabilities and very little energy on our assets, because it seems that when things are not going well, it makes more sense to try to not fail. In other words, try to avoid your liabilities as opposed to building your life around your assets and trying to succeed. So this chapter is a review of assets and liabilities. We'll talk about listing assets and listing liabilities, and then building some goals around those assets. If you have an understanding of your assets, then it also makes it much easier to have positive expectations. In a society in which most of the news programs that people watch are packed with negative things and the papers print negative things and people talk about negative things, it's very, very difficult to get up every day and have positive expectations, especially if these things are only a part of your adversities. If you have a chronic illness, a physical disability or other issues in your life, then all this negative information flooding into your system makes it more difficult to have positive expectations on a daily basis. I feel that this chapter is probably the foundation for the book. If you have a good understanding of this chapter and you're able to use it in your daily life, then you're obviously going to be better prepared for adversity when it comes. And once you have recovered from adversity, then it's always easier to recover the next time around.

The information that you generate in regard to your assets in this chapter will also be beneficial in the chapter which deals with developing a plan and executing that plan on a daily basis.

A better understanding of the value of your assets, and in some cases even the value of your liabilities, gives you a certain sense of comfort when you're able to overcome liabilities. So perhaps one of the messages in this chapter would be that parents need to let children deal with adversity and have failures and have some liabilities. Then when you become an adult, you will obviously be able to deal better with adversity. And everyone—as expressed in the opening chapter—everyone has adversity, everyone has liabilities, everyone has mud in the water, and the better we are able to understand how we receive and process information and how to selectively illuminate some of that information before it gets to the processing stage, then the better we're going to be in regard to executing behaviors on a daily basis. There are three sections to this chapter. One is to recognize the assets and abilities. Two is to understand how we process information and, three, would be to use your knowledge of your assets to develop positive expectations. Take some time and list your assets and then take time and list your liabilities. When you have these two lists, what you find is that the liabilities are the things that take most of your energy when you're involved with adversity. Secondly, you're going to find that perhaps you've taken some assets for granted and some of those assets probably haven't been thought of for a very, very long time. After you have looked at those two lists, look at the liability list and do one of two or three things with that list. Number 1, when you look at the list of liabilities, decide which of those liabilities are just going to be a part of your life, because life is not always rosy and some liabilities are just a part of our existence. Determine which liabilities are going to be a part of your life. Learn to live with those liabilities and develop some assets to perhaps enable those liabilities to be less controlling in your life. Number 2, decide which liabilities you can eliminate. Some of those liabilities will be environmental liabilities, some of which are intangible things and some of those liabilities will be things that can be eliminated by having other people deal with them. The third thing is to decide which liabilities can be turned into assets. You are going to have some things on both lists. Very often, in dealing with athletes, you find that one liability is being emotional. Being emotional is a part of being successful. Athletes realize over time that physical talent will only take them so far in their particular sport, after which time, they have to supplement that talent with positive emotion. And so emotion is a very, very strong asset. On the list of liabilities, many of those same athletes have emotions because if you go over the mental edge emotionally, then emotions become liabilities. That will be discussed in a later chapter, but it's very, very important to know that there are many things that can be on both lists and that it's your responsibility to decide where you want to put it and how you want to use it. Aggression is another factor that may be on both lists. Your team members, people around you who influence your behavior and who help you, can be on both lists. Several of these factors that influence how well you are going to do or how successful you're going to be in your life, can be a bit confusing because there are probably some contradictions. They are, indeed, on both lists. It's not always cut and dry, especially for people with chronic illness; people like me who have multiple sclerosis. Emotion is a tremendous asset for me when I get up in the morning, if I use that emotion to have positive expectations. If I get up in the morning and I'm frustrated and emotion takes over, then emotion is a detriment to my day. So it's my responsibility to use emotion in a positive way. There are several examples that you can review that will give you a better idea of how assets and liabilities impact your everyday behavior. For example, a list of assets from an athlete would be as follows:

1. Strength;
2. Size;
3. Determination;
4. Perseverance;
5. Desire to win;
6. Hard work;
7. A change-up (for those who are not baseball folks, it's a type of pitch);
8. Coach-ability (being able to make adjustments).
9. Next on this athlete's list are gifts from God.
10. A Christian heart on life and baseball.
11. "I think a lot and I'm a good thinker."

Now, if you look at the list of liabilities for that same person, you have:

1. I think a lot. (Which was the last asset on the list);
2. Low confidence in myself and what I do;
3. Too hard on myself;
4. Perfectionism;
5. Another type of pitch, curve ball inconsistent;
6. Worries about hurting my arm. (In this particular case, this athlete had had tendonitis in his arm before and had not really gotten over the mental hurdle of letting himself pitch. He was still worried about hurting his arm every time he pitched.)
7. I doubt my abilities, I don't trust my arm.

8. Nervous when facing good hitters and good teams.

Well, if you look at both of those lists, they are both strong. The asset list is incredibly strong. And the liability list is also very specific and strong. Actually there are probably only two or three liabilities and all the rest on that list of liabilities are just symptoms of those two or three. When you look at your list of liabilities, evaluate the list, be honest when you write the list, don't put it in any priority order. After the list is completed, look at the list and try to decide where the core issues are, and then how many of those other things on the list are symptoms of those issues. On our example of liabilities, one of the core issues is being a perfectionist. If you are a perfectionist then you tend to doubt your abilities, you tend to be nervous if you think you're not going to do well, you're too hard on yourself and you have a low level of self-confidence and you think too much. Those are all symptoms of being a perfectionist. Another core issue on that list was "worries about hurting his arm." That's obviously a mental issue that deals with his physical well-being. That's a core issue. And the last core issue dealt with velocity, inability to throw the ball fast. If you analyze that list of liabilities and decide which ones you can eliminate, which ones you can move over to assets, you only really have three liabilities out of over ten liabilities that you had listed. There are only three and those three can be dealt with. Now, what you do after your assets and liabilities are listed and after you evaluate them, then you should sit and list your goals in the order of the things that you want to accomplish. With goals, there are four things that are very, very important.

1. Goals need to be specific;

2. They need to be difficult because you need to stretch your system everyday to accomplish more;

3. They need to have a timeline attached to them so that you have a certain time in order to evaluate what you have done and what you haven't done; and

4. Perhaps the most important criteria is that they be attainable. The reason for the attainable goal is if you set goals and those goals are based on what you were able to do before you had your adversity—before you got the mud in the water—if you base your goals on previous accomplishments, then you are setting yourself up to have psychological down turn. After you've had adversity, after you've had mud in the water, after you've had to deal with negative things, then your goals should change—at least temporarily change. For example, with MS, if I ran three miles a day, four or five days a week, that would be a worthy goal now. But since I was diagnosed with MS, I don't have the balance and energy to do that. Because fatigue and heat are major issues with MS, I can't sustain for three miles; but I feel like I can go a half mile. If I set my goal to go three miles and I have to stop after a half mile, I'm going to criticize myself and beat myself up because I didn't go three. I should be grateful that I went a half mile, and perhaps in a week or two weeks or three weeks I can go three quarters of a mile. So you begin to build on your revised assets. If I had set my goal as three

miles and at a half mile I knew that I wasn't going to go much further and at that point I lower my goal, then psychologically I'm devastated. It would be much better to set my goal at a quarter of a mile and raise it to a half mile. What I am looking at when I look at assets and abilities and how they relate to goals, is being realistic with myself; being honest with myself. These lists are really nobody's business except your own. They should be a guide for how you begin to recover and how quickly you can recover from adversity. One thing that you're going to find is that once you have your assets and liabilities identified and you have established some short-term goals (don't worry about long-term goals at this time), then you can further allocate your energy. It has always been very, very amusing to me that companies write five-year goals and they re-write them every year. Don't get wrapped up in tying your whole life to long-term goals. Take day by day and have a goal every single day. Something else to remember: put your goals on paper. Write the goals down every day. When you write them and have the goals on paper, you become psychologically tied to them. If you keep them in your head, in your mind, and something more fun comes along, then you could push them to the back and nobody saw them. So you're not accountable for them. If you put them on paper where you can see them in the morning, then you will become attached to them psychologically and you will attempt to achieve those goals. At the end of the day you will have something to look at and to reward yourself if you achieved them and to figure how to do them differently if you didn't achieve them. So it's very, very important that you write them down and that you be honest with your capabilities. After you have listed these three areas, liabilities, assets, and goals, then you should move to listing your self-expectations. In other words, what do I expect from myself personally or professional ly? It's very interesting when you have athletes or corporate people sit and list self-expectations. It's very interesting what you find and it gives you, if you pay attention to those lists, a realistic opportunity to use your assets to accomplish something and to know when you accomplished it.

The final part of this chapter is essential. Without positive expectations, assets and liabilities will not help you that much in recovering from adversity and categorizing important things in your mind. Positive expectations are many times overplayed and not explained to people. Many times, they are not understood. In fact, when people leave jobs, the primary reason over the last ten or fifteen years has not been money or position. The primary reason people have left jobs voluntarily is that they don't know what's expected of them in the work place. It's essential that you use your assets and liabilities to match your expectations so that you can accomplish success. Now that you've listed the assets and liabilities and we've talked about the process of dealing with each of those lists, it's critical that we spend some time talking about expectations.

Expectations, I think, are the foundation for achieving what you want to do in life. We are raised and trained from birth to respond to negative expectations. In fact, by the time an average person is 18 years old, they have been told 185,000 to 200,000 times what not to do growing up in the home and in the educational environment, and not maliciously and not in a threatening way. When we are told "No," something is wrong, then we're supposed to be able to figure out how to do something correctly and that's not always the case. So we grow up and we go out into the world assuming that if we don't fail, that if we avoid failure, that we'll succeed. And that is an incorrect assumption. In order to achieve success, you have to pursue success. You're never going to succeed in life by always moving away from negative things without a positive place to go. In other words, if you're going to achieve something positive, you have to pursue a positive direction. You can't achieve positive things by avoiding a negative direction, because there are too many negative directions available to you and only a couple of positive directions.

It is essential that you have goals that have been discussed in this chapter. It's essential that you understand your assets. And it's essential that you build your path to success around your assets and your goals. In order to do that, you have to expect that you're going to succeed. At least with positive expectations, the probability is on your side that you will succeed and that's probably one of the most important things. Negative expectations would be trying to not miss a free throw in basketball. Positive expectations would be to expect to hit the free throw. At least if you expect to make the free throw, the probability is on your side. It's very frustrating sometimes to see people just surviving in their lives without ever pursuing anything positive; surviving just by avoiding negative things. To me, that's a very superficial way to live your life. Expectations come in all shapes and forms and sizes and it's your responsibility to decide which expectations are realistic and possible for you. Unrealistic expectations are devastating. It's like unrealistic goals. They are devastating psychologically. So expect good things, but expect things that are possible to achieve.

I know that living with MS as I do, expectations change on a daily basis. I expect to walk a half mile tomorrow and if I wake up tomorrow and am not able to get outside and to do that, then it's a negative thing, but I will hold onto that expectation for the next day. In other words, it's not devastating to me. It doesn't drive me crazy that I can't do it on that particular day. People with chronic illnesses and physical disabilities need to have specific expectations, but at the same time, need to be flexible. I think that to expect to go out and "do the best I can" should be avoided at all costs, because it's not specific. If I'm going to expect to do the best I can, and I get up in the morning and I can't walk at all for an hour or two, then I achieved something because all I wanted to do was the best I could—and that was the best I could do. That makes no sense to me. We need to have goals that drive us every day to achieve things. And if we meet our expectations, if we achieve our goals every day and we use our assets to do that, then we should reward ourselves at the end of the day for achieving something. The only thing that is going to drive a person to continue to pursue expectations and goals and to pursue constructive views of their assets is that they reward themselves at the end of the day. If they set out to do something during a certain time period, say one day, and at the end of that one day their goals are achieved, they need to reward themselves.

We need to be recognized for good achievement. If I remember in dealing with athletes for the last 39 years, that it makes no difference how much athletes make, whether it's a million, 5 million, 10 million, 15 million, at the end of a game in which they have performed well, they still want to be told that they had a good game. It's not about money. It's about the spirit, it's about being competitive, it's about wanting to achieve, it's about self-fulfillment, and they want to be recognized for accomplishing those things. The same thing is true for a person with an illness, a person who struggles to walk. If all of a sudden they walk for 30 minutes and the most they've walked in a week is 15 minutes, then that deserves recognition. And if there's no one around to recognize you for that achievement, then you need to recognize yourself. You need to have a reward, you need to give yourself something that is an indication that you achieved something special during that particular time. You can't really reward yourself unless you have very specific expectations, very specific goals, and a clear understanding of what you set out to achieve in the first place. So when you begin to understand that mud in the water is merely a description of having a cluttered mind and that everybody has it, you have to decide for yourself what is important to keep in your mind, what's important to get rid of, and what's important to store. The bottom line is to use your assets to recover quicker from adversity; use your assets to achieve. Use your assets to help you accomplish the goals that you have set out for yourself.

Once that is done and you have an understanding of this concept, then you are ready to move on to surrounding yourself with the right people, to having a team around you that supports you. You are able to develop a plan and you are able to really understand the role of emotions as a supplement to your assets. To recognize your assets, use the worksheets at the end of this chapter. Recognize your liabilities, understand that your goal here is to develop your life around your assets which makes it easier for you to recover quickly from adversity and recognize that there are other people around you who can offset some of your liabilities and then move ahead with your life with positive expectations.

ASSETS
(LIST IN NO PRIORITY ORDER)

1. _____

2. _____

3. _____

4. _____

5. _____

6. _____

7. _____

8. _____

9. _____

10. _____

LIABILITIES

(LIST IN NO PRIORITY ORDER)

1. _____

2. _____

3. _____

4. _____

5. _____

6. _____

7. _____

8. _____

9. _____

10. _____

ACTION PLAN:
TO USE ASSETS AND ELIMINATE LIABILITIES

ASSET ACTIONS:

1. _____

2. _____

3. _____

4. _____

5. _____

LIABILITY ACTIONS:

1. _____

2. _____

3. _____

4. _____

5. _____

CHAPTER 3

Develop a Plan, But be Flexible

To this point in the text, we've recognized the "mud in the water" which everybody has, mud that's both clutter and good information. We've organized our assets and liabilities. We've talked about setting goals and expectations and we've talked about putting a team in place which is based on needs. Now, it's time to talk about a plan. I don't know of any situation that I've ever been associated with which has not been executed based on a plan. Many times we do things in our lives and consciously don't realize that we have a plan in place, because we never sit to talk about it or write it down. The reality is there's almost always a plan; not always a good plan, but some kind of plan in place. It's critical that if you want to "get the mud out of the water," if you want to clear your mind and move ahead with your life, you need a plan. You need a plan that everybody understands. You need a plan that is relatively simple, logical and sequential, and a plan that's based on your goals. You set your goals and whether those goals are weekly, monthly or yearly goals, and it's always a good idea after you've established goals to work backwards. In other words, if you have a goal for 12 months out, then what do you want to accomplish within 6 months, or within 3 months, or within 1 month and then back that further so that you know what you want to do every single day that leads to the success of the plan and achievement of the goals you've set. We'll talk later in this chapter about pitfalls. Real life dictates there are pitfalls in almost every situation and we'll talk about how to get through those in executing your plan. For example, many times people get caught in traffic and there's no backup plan. You have plans to get to your destination, but there's no flexibility in that plan. When people drive through Atlanta, Georgia on their way to Florida, their plan is to get off of 75 South onto 285 South, drive around Atlanta, get back on 75 and continue south. In reality, the best plan is to drive 75 straight through the city, because no trucks are allowed to pass through Atlanta. Consequently, if you take 285, you run into all the truck traffic. So every plan needs some flexibility for the best outcome.

Plans are not carved in stone. Plans are good, but the most important thing to remember when you put a plan together is that you need to make sure you're able to execute the plan. Anyone can make a plan. That's not the issue. The issue is having the talent or the people around you that enable you to accomplish your plan. Many times, plans are very well organized, but many times we don't take the extra step which requires that we match the plan with our assets and goals, and make sure we have the right team members in place for the plan to be successful. There are many examples that I've encountered over the years, especially in working with athletes. Probably the best pitcher that I've ever seen in 39 years had a plan for every game. That's right, every single game he had a plan regarding what he was going to execute and when he would execute it. He would save certain pitches for later in a game to a good hitter. It was incredible to watch him execute his plan every five days. What people don't realize is that there were four days consumed to put that plan together. He did it very well and won over 350 games in baseball which, if you are a baseball fan you know, is near impossible. The point being that not only was he a good pitcher, but he had a plan. He had a plan that meshed well with his talent. He didn't over pitch and he didn't try things he wasn't capable of doing. He planned every single pitch, and the execution was for a purpose, and he never veered from that plan. It was fun to watch. In almost any situation you could think of, there's been a plan in place. For salespeople in a corporate environment, there should always be a plan, and within that plan there needs to be flexibility, a plan B, plan C. The important thing is that most of your energy is spent executing the plan, not trying to avoid pitfalls within that plan. As a public speaker, I always have a plan in place. When I am booked to speak for a corporation, I get as much information as possible from the internet regarding the company. After that, I talk with key people in the company and get a feel for where they are. Where they are in productivity, where their expectations are and where what they have accomplished in the past year. The next step is to go to the meeting early and to sit in on sessions of the meeting to get a feel for the mood of the group, whether they are anxious, whether they are happy, and that's the basis on where my speech is situated within the agenda. Obviously, if I'm first on the agenda, then I have to be flexible within my plan and talk to more people before the meeting starts. If I'm in the second or third day of the meeting, then my next step is to find out from those in charge of the meeting what goes on before my meeting. Are the people going to be complimented on their performance? Are they going to be challenged, or are the goals going to be the same for the next year? Do they feel the goals are realistic or unrealistic? I try to find their security level within the group before I speak. I try to get a feel for the demographics in the meeting, males, females, experience level, age range. Then the next step is to go to the meeting room, check the mike, make sure everything works, walk around the room, go to the back of the room to see if I can see the stage and make sure there's not anywhere on the stage that's not visible to everyone in the group. Then I talk with the media folks at the meeting to see if they are going to be recording the meeting in order to see where the cameras are going to be. Once all that is done, I make sure a printed introduction is given to the person who will be in charge of introducing me. I try to sit and spend time with that person before the meeting, because the most frustrating thing to happen in a meeting is when there's no introductory material and you're introduced as "here's the speaker." Then you have to spend the first part of the meeting selling the group on your credentials and then get into the content of the meeting. This is a waste of time, so I try to have all that material in order before I address the group. I find out how much time I have to speak and if there's any flexibility in that time for questions and answers. So there are a lot of things that go on in an hour long meeting that most people in the group do not realize take place. I remember a few years ago I was speaking at a meeting in Las Vegas. I went in the day before the meeting and it was a major international convention. I went to the room the night before and spent four to five hours sitting behind the stage with the engineers watching them put it together in order to get a feel for those folks and their commitment to what the meeting entailed, and all the things they had to go through to prepare the stage for my speech. It gave me a comfort and peace of mind to know that everything was going to be in place. So if you want to be successful at whatever you do, you need to do your homework. You need to make sure that you have the tools needed. If I need for example, a cordless mike, if I need to move around, then I need to make sure it's available the day before the meeting as opposed to waiting until an hour before the speech. After the speech, the evaluation process begins. How was the presentation absorbed, how was the style received? Was the content of the meeting relevant? Did it relate directly to that company? All those things are very important in the evaluation process not only to understand the feedback from the meeting, but to prepare for future meetings. At this point, it would be a help to anyone who's planning to review a series of questions that I always review when planning to execute, whether it's a speech or whether it's a program with athletes; no matter what situation I'm in, I try to answer these questions before I start.

The big questions are:

1. Where do you want to go? In other words, when your plan is in place, where do you want that plan to take you?

2. What are the peripheral influences on you and the program? Are there distractions that are unavoidable in the room? I spoke at one meeting in which there were big columns in the room. Not everyone in the audience could see so I had to make sure in my plan that I was flexible. I had to make sure that as I spoke I moved around the room so that everyone at some point was able to see the presentation. People relate more to it if they can see it, touch it and feel it. That question needs to be answered whether it's a personal plan of execution, or whether it's a personal plan.

3. What's your timeline? How long do you have to execute this plan so that you give yourself plenty of time and you do your due diligence in planning for the execution? I remember when I was a professor at a university, I always joked with students that on a semester system they had to study two times a year and on the quarter system they had to study three times a year. It was a joke, but it was interesting in that when you assign projects and you give students ten weeks to do the project, how many students work an hour a day for ten weeks as opposed to the number of students who start the project the week that it's due or even, in some cases, the day before it's due. It's so important that when you have that ten-week period to execute you're able again to work backwards on your goals so that you have something every day that will lead you to success in your plan.

4. How do you evaluate yourself? In other words, after the plan is completed, what's the evaluation process? How successful was it? What can be done to the plan to make it more successful the next time? It's very important to note here that you need to be accountable. You establish your plan, surround yourself with the right people, establish the assets that are needed, the talents that are needed to execute the plan and then the execution takes place. So you need to be realistic as to what did or did not happen during the execution of the plan. It's the only way to have an honest evaluation with yourself and be able to improve.

5. How do others evaluate you? In some instances the evaluation process, at least in sales, might be whether or not you close the deal. If you close the deal, then the plan is looked at as a success. Sometimes this is correct and sometimes not. In education, if your grades are good, then the plan was executed well. In a speech, if the audience responds favorable, then the evaluation at least initially is good. So there's always a way to evaluate the execution of your plan. There's always a way to determine in an objective way whether or not you were successful. If you let emotion take over your evaluation, then there's always enough blame to go around if the plan was not executed well. So again, nothing is stronger here than being accountable for what you've just put in place.

6. Are you totally committed to getting better? The only reason you would evaluate a plan and evaluate it honestly is

if you want to become better. For those folks who just want to get it over with or just "get through it", you will never get much better because you've merely survived. As we've talked about in this book and will continue to discuss, there's a big difference between those who want to win and be successful and those who just want to survive. So survival is a very dangerous posture to have when you're trying to execute a plan.

7. Perhaps the most critical question is: Why do I do this? In other words, why do I do what I do? It would be difficult for me to be committed to a plan if I did not really understand why I do what I do. It's a tough question to answer. It's needs to be based on intrinsic motivation and incentives as opposed to getting a fee for executing the plan. It needs to go much further than that and, in my case, I evaluate my performance based on whether or not I was able to emotionally touch people. For example, take when I talk to a group of MS patients. As we've talked about before Multiple Scerosis is a very devastating, unpredictable disease without a cure. When I have a hundred MS patients in a room, I have at least two goals in mind. Number 1 is to get those people back in touch with their emotions, because many times with this disease, when people are diagnosed, they give up. They lose the emotions that they've always had. They lose the very things that make them who they are. So my plan is to have at least a few people in the audience laugh and cry within an hour. My belief is that if you laugh and cry within the same

hour, then you've gotten back in touch with your emotions. It's now your choice to use those emotions to make yourself better. If not physically, at least emotionally. Now, those are seven questions that I think are critical to executing a plan and if you can answer all those questions honestly and plan on answer all those questions, then you are going to be much more effective in your execution. This year in a professional baseball environment, I had a pitching coach ask me to work with a couple of pitchers. My question is the same every time I'm asked. Number 1, do they want to win? Are they committed to success? Being told that there were, my next question was obvious. What are the issues that we're dealing with? The coach had a very interesting comment. He said they have tremendous talent, they know how to play the game, they love the game, but they don't have a plan. It was interesting because who would think that a professional athlete would not have a plan? But during the heat of battle or during the heat of a sales meeting or a conversation with your children, it's easy to let emotion take over, then the plan goes south and you're not really able to get it back. So with that in mind, we sat down and we put plans together. I let them put the plan together and I was there to help them, not only to execute the plan, but to plan for negative events. If something that's negative happens, how do we recover quickly and get back to the plan? You see, quick recovery is necessary to execute the plan in a timely fashion. Anybody can recover over time if they are persistent in the task. The question is not whether or not they can recover; the question is how quickly can they recover? If a pitcher can recover between pitches as opposed to between innings, then obviously the outcome is going to be much more favorable. So we put a plan in place and these guys performed very well and seemed to be able to use their energy better because there was very little wasted energy in their performance.

Now, let's talk for a second about the pitfalls that occur during execution. In any plan, you have to be flexible because there are always possible pitfalls to "get the mud out of the water."

Now it needs to be said here that you can never execute a plan trying to avoid pitfalls. In other words, if you're trying to avoid pitfalls in your performance, then basically, you're executing to not lose which is a survivor mentality and very unproductive. So you always plan to be successful. We talked about expectations. You always have to expect to be successful to put the probability of success on your side. It's human nature to think sometimes about the pitfalls and we don't try to avoid that. When you think about the possible pitfalls, before you execute any further in the plan you need to go back and visualize something successful that you've executed before in the plan, and then set out to succeed. So you've basically replaced the cautious negative expectations with a positive outlook on performance. There are mental blocks that might take place. Many times when you are executing a plan, you can get so engrossed in the performance that you forget to take a mental break. Everyone, because our neuro-

logical systems are set up this way, tries to execute on a consistent basis when things are going well. We need to take
time, whether it's 20 seconds, or ten seconds, or a minute.
We have to take periodic mental breaks. I call these timed
mental lapses. Do you have a mental lapse during a critical
performance or do you have a mental lapse when you want
to have it in between episodes of performance? It's obviously
better to have a mental lapse when you want to have a mental break. So take a mental break periodically through the
performance. That can be a real problem if you become emotionally fatigued. It may be because you haven't really given
yourself a break.

I worked with a professional poker player a few years
ago. We looked at several tournaments to try to determine
where during the day he could take mental breaks. On the
last day of a tournament, sometimes you're at the head table.
If you're one of the final ten, you're at the head table for up
to 14 hours. That's the reason so many younger players are
winning the tournaments. It's not that they are better players than the older players; it's that they have more endurance
than the older players. So we picked out times during the
tournament that this player could take 20 seconds here, 20
seconds there and rejuvenate his system. This allowed him
to have more energy later in the performance. You watch
sports teams all the time that may play three great quarters
of football, for example, and get blown away in the fourth
quarter. Many times it's not physical fatigue; it's mental
fatigue because they haven't given themselves a break during
the first three quarters. So anytime you're not on the firing
line, anytime you're not in the game, anytime you not

involved directly in the meeting, then many times you have time to give yourself a short mental break. If you don't take a mental break during the execution of the plan, then peripheral things will begin to seem much more significant. In other words, you're not able to hold selective attention or focus. You begin to notice things and react to cues in the environment that have nothing to do with performance. So when a person loses their focus, many times it's because they are fatigued mentally. They have gotten too much mud in the water and by that I mean all of a sudden they have ten times the number of things on their mind than they should have. During the course of a performance, basically you've shut your system down. It makes recovery take longer and it makes recovery much more difficult. So mental fatigue is a real issue that doesn't have to be an issue at all if you just give yourself a planned break. You may have to change strategies during the execution of a plan. That's a challenge, but that's one of those things that may be perceived as a pitfall and it's not. It's strength, because if you have to change strategies during the course of your plan, then it makes you much better the next time you have to execute the plan. That's another reason for doing your due diligence before you ever start the execution.

You also need to avoid the pitfall caused by lack of time management. Time management is a necessary process. We don't as a rule do a very good job with time management. It's been said that during an eight hour day, if you really good you may get over six hours of productivity, maybe seven. It's also been said that if you work a 13 hour day and you're good, you get seven hours of productivity. What I'm saying here is that it's so easy to be distracted and veer from your plan that it could take twice the time to execute. So we don't need to set out by doing a task based on unlimited time. What we need to do early on is to look at the situation, determine how much time we have and then plan to get the most productivity out of that time.

We've also talked a little bit about the possible physical pitfalls to plan execution. I think these are obvious to most people or should be. You need to be physically able, obviously, to execute. Nothing can be more devastating to any performance than a lack of energy. That comes many times from over-thinking, panic, or anxiety based on the execution. All those things are discussed in this book. Nutrition is many times an issue as is lack of exercise. When you are executing any plan, it's very important that you take care of all the physical issues related to your health.

There are sometimes team pitfalls. Maybe you have the wrong people in place. Maybe certain team members feel like they are not being used properly. There are always things that can happen. But you should be prepared for those, not dwell on them. Be prepared for them when they come. That's just a part of setting up the plan and structuring the plan. You need to realize that here are some things that have happened in the environment before, but again, before you execute, you don't forget those pitfalls, but again you think of things and visualize things that have gone well during previous executions. That will get you on the road to being successful. It's very important that you keep in mind what you are doing, why you are doing it and what you hope the outcome will be.

We've talked about motivation before. Motivation is obviously important, but the most important thing about motivation is to be achievement motivated. There's no better way to be achievement motivated than to have specific goals and a specific plan in place that drives you to achieve.

In summary, I would say it's critical once you have the structure in place that you practice, practice, and practice. Practice execution, practice conversations. Visualize. Visualize success. In working with professional golfers it's interesting to me that on Tuesdays before a tournament they always have a practice round. During that practice round, you really learn how important the caddy is to the execution of the plan. The caddies know where every tree is on the course; they know which way the grass grows, whether you're putting with the grain or against the grain. They know all the breaks on the greens. They know the type of sand in the traps. They know the thickness and texture of it. They know the different types of rough and what kind of grass is in the rough. They record all that in a book and when the player plays in the tournament, if you will notice, they always talk with the caddy before a shot. Many times they will pull out the book and they'll begin to use hand motions. They decide where they want to go with the shot and how high to hit the ball. They determine the wind direction and intensity. With this information, they can plan every single shot throughout the day based on those factors. And so the caddy is a very important part of the team. I think that example is good for realizing how important it is to have good people around you, and to pay attention to the environmental factors that might influence your execution.

PERSONAL TEAM STRUCTURE

TALENT/ASSETS NEEDED:

1. _____

2. _____

3. _____

4. _____

5. _____

PLAYERS:

1. _____

2. _____

3. _____

4. _____

5. _____

CHAPTER 4

Have Go-To Players on Your Team

Over the past several years, I've had more requests for speeches dealing with teamwork than probably any other topic. Everybody refers to their team. Corporations refer to teams. In education, we have teams. Everybody refers to teams in one way or another. Winners recognize the importance of the team concept. They know they need to be members of the team, to support the team, and also to be supported by the team. They know where they fit and understand their roles on the team. The biggest barrier to recognizing or realizing the value of a team is confusion about role definition, or maybe just a lack of role definition. What is it that you as a team member are supposed to do? Again, the reason most people give for leaving a company is that they don't know what's expected. That is, they don't know or understand their role on the team. Personally, that's also true. A lot of people who you would like to have on your team may be willing, but in order for them to be effective on your team, you have to have a conversation about team roles, about expectations, about the things that are important to you and your vision in order to have those team members be effective. As you define your team for winning every day, which everyone should do, professionally or personally, you need to describe where you want to go and what you want to accomplish. Once you've communicated this information, then you need other team members who compliment and support your talents. This is crucial to the team's success and therefore to your success. If you're team has only point guards, for example, then all you do is pass the ball around and nobody scores. In other words, if team members are there just to support people and never to challenge you, then you don't accomplish very much. If you're team has only shooters then there's nobody to throw the ball in, so you lose either way. On your team, you need leaders and supporters. You need people who are going to take risk and people who are going to support the risk-takers. Sometimes, you have to do both. In the same situation every employee must feel not only important, but critical to the team's performance or to the productivity of the team. Every player needs something to which he or she can be attached personally, something to which he or she can make a genuine contribution. In sports, every player must feel critical to the outcome of the game or to the team's status as a winner. In the family, parents must feel critical to the development of their children. With MS, I need every team member to recognize my vision. I need every team member to recognize my disabilities, to recognize where I need help. I need every team member to be willing to help me basically get the mud out of the water. Everything we do is basically a team effort, even though many times we feel alone. Even in individual sports, there's always a team involved. There's always a support system There's always someone who understands the goals and the desired outcomes and then tries to contribute to achieving those goals and attaining the outcomes. You don't always see the other team members, but they are there. Team-building first, followed by teamwork is an essential concept for winning, both personally and professionally. On your team, you first need to identify and understand what it is you want to accomplish and whether or not a team is important to achieving your goals. I can't think of any situation where a team would not be needed. Then you must determine what members your team needs and the role of each person on your team and the expectations and accountability of the members of the team. As indicated in the title of this chapter, you need go-to players, you need team members who are available to you on-call, team members who are supportive and team members who are challenging. The process of forming your team requires you to 1) Evaluate your goals; 2) Review your assets and liabilities, and 3) Make sure that you have not only team members who support your assets, but also team members who offset your liabilities. You need to determine the team talents that are needed. You also need to select additional team members with needed assets. Lastly, you need to select team members who are committed to helping you. If you have a chronic illness such as MS, you can find plenty of team members who are going to support you, plenty of team members who are going to give you sympathy, but it's also necessary to have team members who are going to challenge you to do things. They know where you want to go, what your goals are, and they will try to make sure they help you achieve those goals. So the most critical factor is to make sure that the team functions properly. Team members participate and they contribute at different times based on your needs. Of course, all team members are available when needed. Remember that it only takes one individual on the team to cause the team to lose. Have you ever observed a situation where everyone has a good attitude before one negative person walks in and within 15 minutes, the whole team is down? You have to separate yourself and your team from that kind of a team-wrecker. Eliminating having such a person around will automatically improve the probability that your team will succeed. The cliché that is very appropriate here is that it only takes one rotten apple to spoil the whole bushel. I remember one person I worked with a few years ago who had several team members who supported what she did and what she wanted to accomplish. Then, almost overnight, one team member decided to take control and decide what she thought was best for the whole team. As opposed to being a support person, she took on the role of being the leader and made the team all about her. It didn't take long for the team to become disrupted and very dysfunctional. My advice was really simple: eliminate that person from the team. It doesn't mean that they are a bad person, and it doesn't mean that they don't have good intentions. In this case, it just meant that she didn't fit in that particular team concept. Once that person was eliminated, the team came back together and the person who established the team as a support system became very successful. What you should put in place when you're forming your team is something that should be enduring, something that's going to be there every day. People will see it, people will feel it, and people will want to be a part of it. It's there if you make changes to your team. In other words, the concept, the "Team Concept", is the enduring factor. It needs to be related to your philosophy of a team, your goals for your team, and the foundation of the team. It must be capable of living through even the most dramatic changes of the team. The basic winning chemistry of the team must still be there because you must still have the same basic philosophy that you had when you started. That concept should be what keeps the team engine running smoothly. Now, change on the team is something that is natural. Changes are not always comfortable, but they to be made on occasion for the good of the whole team. Change can be exciting and it can be rewarding. Variation in the team's makeup can produce tremendous results if it's done for the right reasons and the goals are kept paramount. In families, you must have the dramatic changes that occur in sports, but there are still times that will test your philosophy and your goals. But if the basic concepts are what they should be, then you must hold on to them. You must keep them out front and you must strive towards those goals every single day without fail. You must be able to call on team members when you veer off track, so then you are in a winning mode. In almost every team, whether it's personal or professional, there are going to be conflicts. To be a winning team does not mean that the team members have to love each other. It means that they have to respect each others' assets and liabilities and they have to play in a coordinated way. Conflicts are part of the equation and in many cases they make a team stronger, especially if they are resolved. Conflict can be a positive thing if it causes change and risk taking, which are good for the team. Recognition of the contributions of team members is essential. It's very important that when team members do things for the good of the team which may challenge you, or you might initially disagree with, it's very important that you recognize those contributions. This is true for every kind of team, whether it's your personal team, your family team or your corporate team. There's a good example that I've used many times and probably used in ever book that I've written about what I consider to be the consummate team concept. One of my most enjoyable experiences came when I spoke at a company's annual employee appreciation meeting around 2000. Every team member from the cleanup crew to the chairman of the board attended. Everyone received recognition for his or her contributions to helping the corporate team win and it was a major winner. All the other team members knew each other by name, regardless of their status within the company. Talking with those team members and watching them interact, I could easily see that they shared a strongly coordinated work effort and common goals. The team had what I consider to be a winning chemistry. There was another example I had in working with a sports team in which chemistry was never emphasized; it wasn't a major factor on the team. The team was made up of very talented athletes, but it was not a team. There were no support players. The players were a group of individuals who played under a team name and they were not successful. Another team I worked with in the racing industry had a similar situation because the crew members were not recognized by the leaders of the team. There was no positive re-enforcement. Everyone was trying to not fail, everyone was very self conscious about the security or insecurity of their job, and so therefore that team was not successful. So there are basic things that every team has to have in order to be successful. I think probably the most important is the team chemistry. Team chemistry is one of those things we never talk about until we don't have it. I remember one year while working with a professional baseball team, the team lost ten games in a row. So they come back later and they win ten in a row. One of the players was asked, "How's the team chemistry after a ten game winning streak?" The player responded by saying, "Chemistry is overrated. We go out and we play every day and we play to win." This was interesting because later in that same year, they lost nine games in a row. The same player was questioned, "What's wrong with the team?" His response was, "We lost our chemistry." So chemistry is one of those things we don't talk about until we don't have it. On your team, you need members who are supporting players, you need others who are independent, others who are adventurous, others who are aggressive risk-takers and others who want to be in control. To make it the consummate team, you need diversity. So the team doesn't just consist of your friends. The team consists of people who are going to enable you to be successful. I've always said that the consummate coach is one who creates an environment that has good chemistry in which the players can play the game, not feel intimidated and make the coach look good. Once the team is assembled, members must understand their team personality and philosophy. They must understand the team's goals and what they mean to each individual player. They need to know what resources are available to reach the goals, and then they need to understand what happens when they reach the goals as a team. Let's use golf as an example. A golfer is typically seen as an individual sport performer, but little do people realize how many people are involved on a golf team for a specific golfer. I worked with a professional golfer a few years ago who was a great player, and who was recognized as being a great player. But on his team he had me as a sports psychologist, he had a weight-training and development person, he had a nutritionist, he had a driving coach, a middle iron coach, he had a putting coach, he had an agent, he had a marketing person, and he had a PR person. All of those people were critical to the team and his success, but none of those people are ever recognized for being a part of a golfer's life. But without that team, the golfer would be unsuccessful. Now, there are different types of teams. You might want to surround yourself with people who are members of your social team. These are the people who, if you're prone to not be a social person, these are the people who cause you to be active.

They make sure you attend events; they make sure you meet people and these are important people on your social team. Then you have a work team, and the work team many times is the people who lend emotional support, team members who are action oriented, team members who obviously offset your liabilities and also team members who supplement your assets. To use a very specific example, since I was diagnosed with MS a few years ago so I've established what I think is a team that has enabled me to stay relatively healthy and also to remain productive. It's very easy when you have a situation in your life where you're diagnosed with a disease that is obviously a devastating disease for which there is no cure. It's very easy to be emotionally down. It's easy to crawl in a hole and to avoid contact with people. But early on after I was diagnosed, I established my team. My team members may seem unusual, but they were good for me. Everybody needs a team that's good for them. One of my team members was Bobby Cox, the former Atlanta Braves manager. Bobby Cox was not only supportive during my four or five years with the Atlanta Braves after my diagnosis, but he had a way of creating an environment where the emphasis was not on the downside of my diagnosis, but rather on the fun side. People accuse me many times of making fun of MS, but that wasn't the case. I accept it for what it is and everybody around me on the Atlanta Braves team accepted it for what it was, and Bobby did also. He was very compassionate, very caring, but at the same time, I've always told people that he was the captain of my team because he never once in those four or five years excused me from doing my job.

y sound strange to some, but it was very effective because it kept my wheels turning. I had so much respect for him that I wouldn't dare not do the job that I was hired to do. It was just understood that that was the way it was supposed to be. I had occasions where I couldn't go to the stadium, or I didn't feel good, or it was too hot. I could have called and said, you know, I'm not coming and he would have said that's fine. But I didn't do that. I credit him for keeping me in a healthy state of mind. One of my other team members is Dr. Ben Thrower. He's a neurologist at the Shepherd Spinal Center in Atlanta. He's my physician and I trust him with my life. People ask me what medications I take and I have no idea what some of them are, but Dr. Thrower prescribed them and I take them. Everybody should have somebody that they trust in that way. I never question what he says to me and what he recommends to me. He's a very important team member. I have other team members. My children, obviously, because they are the reason that I continue to do what I do. They are an inspiration to me and I consider them critical team members. I have friends on my team who call me constantly and check on my health and ask me how I'm doing and tell me to hang in there. Then I have other team members who are friends who challenge me on a daily or weekly basis. When I say to them, "I don't think I can go to lunch," their response is, "Be ready in 15 minutes; we're going to lunch." I always feel better after I do those things. As I've mentioned before, it would be so easy to to feel bad and it's so difficult to feel good. But once you take the step to feel better, and sometimes it takes team members to cause you to take that step, then you're glad you took the risk and also glad you took the chance. I think one of the most critical requirements with team members is that you need team members who actually talk to you. We need to move away from facebooking, texting, twittering, e-mailing and faxing. We need to communicate at least verbally if not face-to-face. It's very important if you realize that 60% or more of communication is non-verbal, then it's virtually impossible to use that 60% if you're texting and you're e-mailing. You need to physically see people. We've used the cliché a few times in this book that what you are talking so loud people can't hear which you say. Basically, this means that people need to see you, your reactions, your eyes, your body, and your posture, how well you're moving around. They need to feel those things and good team members are willing to do that. Perhaps the most important thing that I think you need to do is once you've formed your team, then you need to listen to the team. You need to realize that all the team members are committed to you. They are all on your side. Nobody is going to say something to hurt you or say something to cause you to feel worse. They may say things that challenge you and they may say things that you disagree with, but, in their mind, they're doing it to help you become stronger. Of course, you need to talk with your team members on a regular basis. If you're having issues on Monday, it doesn't do any good to call your team members on Thursday or Friday and tell them how you felt on Monday. If you need your team on Monday, call them on Monday. That's what they're there for. They understand this and you understood it when you picked those people. So use those folks whenever you are in need. Many times if I have mud in the water, if I have too many things on my mind, it really helps to sit down with one of my team members and just talk. I talk about those things and decide which of those things I can eliminate or give to a team member, and decide which ones I have to live with, and then develop a plan to live with those things. And to decide which things that are necessary in my life, but many times I don't need to think about them when I'm working. I need to be able to compartmentalize those things. Team members are invaluable when it comes to helping you sort through the mud in the water. I remember a few years ago, we had a team member that baseball scouts would tell me, "he has no speed, he has no range, his arm's not strong, he's not a great hitter and if he was released today, no other team would sign him to a contract." But they would follow that by saying, "the Atlanta Braves can't win without him." That's the consummate team member. That's the person, the glue that holds the team together. You need one of those people around you, whether in the corporate environment, or a family situation or if you're a person with some disability or a person like me with a chronic illness. You need somebody around you who is going to keep the team together and who's going to pull you back when you veer off course. They know your goals, they know where you're going, they know what you want to achieve and so many of those folks on your team have ideas that might enable you to get there quicker or at least in a less energy consuming way. If that's the case, then you need to utilize those people. Everybody needs a go-to person within the team. You don't need people with individual agendas on your team. You don't want people who are there for the wrong reasons. I've had people tell me that they've had people on their team who are "mothering" people; people who want to feel bad for them. People who want to be their constant security blanket. I think everybody needs a security blanket. Everybody needs somebody around who is going to recognize that you feel bad and be sympathetic to that, but not on a 24-hour a day basis. You need people who are going to be there for you in a support way, but at the same time, again, in a challenging way. NASCAR is a good example of what I consider to be the consummate team. When I do team work seminars for corporations, I always make the comment that if you want to see how a team works, go to a NASCAR race and stand in the pits for one race. You will see five people jump over the wall when the car comes to the pits, fill it up with gas, change four tires, clean off the grill, pull the tear-away for the windshield, get the driver a drink of water and adjust the car in less than 13 seconds. That's an amazing thing to me. In fact, a few years ago when crew members were accomplish those things in less than 13 seconds, they were awarded a cash bonus. Now, almost every crew is able to accomplish those tasks in 13 seconds or less and it's because they respect each other. Many times they have conflicts, but when it's time to go over the wall, they're all on the same team. What I'm saying is when it comes time to go over the wall with you, you need team members who are all on the same page. I've seen examples where that's been true in NASCAR and I've seen examples where that's not true in NASCAR. The latter being when team members were not recognized for what they did, when team members were always insecure about their jobs, and when team members were not recognized by the driver as being important and it lead to very unsuccessful results on that particular team.

In summary, it's very important to:

1. Recognize your assets and your liabilities.

2. Select team members who offset your liabilities and other team members who supplement your assets.

3. Select team members who are committed to helping you reach your jobs.

4. Communicate your goals and aspirations to team members so they understand what you expect from them.

5. Recognize those team members when they do something for you. Nothing more than a comment many times is valuable to team members who are trying their best to make life better for you, so you need to recognize those people on your team. And at some point, it may be weekly, it may be monthly, it may be once a year, but at your discretion at some point you have to have your team together and you have to have some type of recognition around the table for everybody for their contributions to enabling you to become more successful. I would like nothing better than to be able to have all my

team members get together just so I could sit and look at them and recognize all of them. That's not possible, but it doesn't mean that we're not a team. They are spread all over the world, and I know that the ones who don't live close to me are only a phone call away and that's a great feeling. If you decide that you need a team, which I think that everybody does, then you make the commitment to have the team help you.

GOALS

1. _____

2. _____

3. _____

4. _____

5. _____

ACTION PLAN

1. _____

2. _____

3. _____

4. _____

5. _____

Move from Habitual to Perceptual Behaviors

Winners convert habits to perceptual behaviors. Not an easy task, but critical to recovering quicker from adversity. At a very early age, individuals learn basic habits which are necessary to move through life's challenges. A complete list of habits is, of course, beyond the scope of this chapter.

HABITUAL BEHAVIORS

Habitual Behavior: Internal focus using conditioned responses without regard to environmental factors which we consider psychological noise.

In children, habits begin as basic reflexes and progress to conditioned reflexes such as walking, running, throwing and catching. Extracurricular activities provide an environment for refining these physical habits. Classrooms enable students to develop good study habits. Cultural surroundings provide learning opportunities for behavioral and social habits. People are constantly bombarded with the need to have good habits. Young people memorize facts. They regurgitate those facts and score well on tests, make good grades, and consequently develop a false sense of security regarding preparation for a successful life, both personally and professionally. In athletics, there are two types of sports: habitual and perceptual. In habitual sports such as golf, gymnastics, ice skating, swimming, and bowling, habitual execution will ensure a comfortable level of success. In these sports, one tries to execute conditional skills regardless of environmental factors and the skill level of opponents. In the corporate world, salespeople are trained to execute habits. At one recent convention where I was speaking, participants were encouraged to "get back to basic habits." Book store shelves are packed with books promoting habits of successful people. Readers become conditioned to be habitual and may reach a comfortable level of success, the consummate survivor performance level.

Habitual training that makes me most uncomfortable is parent training. It is also a bit uncomfortable knowing that many parenting book authors do not have children. Being a parent of four children, I realized early on that no two children are exactly alike. Therefore raising them cannot be accomplished using parental habits learned in classes. Parenting is the consummate trial and error challenge. As a parent, the more habitual you are, the lower your probability of success. The children who are raised by parents to be perceptual in the environment and who learn to make decisions accordingly, will mature quicker and be more productive adults. In many ways, these examples remind us of animal training. A reminder of Pavlov's dog; hear the bell and salivate. In short, habitual performances may enable one to perform, compete and survive.

This is probably a good plan, if one goes through life free from adversity. The basic flaw in this position is that an adversity-free life is nothing more than a fantasy. This statement is not meant to minimize the necessity of habitual behavior, because habits are, in fact, the very foundation of our journey through life, both personally and professionally. Essentially, the consistent execution of habits only guarantees that people will reach a certain level of performance in all phases of their lives, at which point they will plateau. Progress stops and survival starts.

Winners are the people who desire a higher level of existence. Winners demonstrate the ability to approach every day with the intent of learning more, accomplishing more and getting more fulfillment from life. These are the people who use habits as a platform to become perceptual. You can stop here if you are happy being a creature of habit. If you want to achieve more and reach a higher level of performance and fulfillment, then you need to become perceptual. Every day brings the opportunity to reach beyond the customary routine activities. Adversity, or "mud in the water," necessitates that we use habits to become perceptual.

PERCEPTUAL BEHAVIOR

Perceptual Behavior: Externally focused behavior attending to environmental factors, then responding with appropriate actions, often modifying habitual actions.

At this point in the chapter, it should be obvious that the

most comfortable lifestyle is one of consistent, habitual execution. The basic problem with this hypothesis is that environmental factors, "psychological noise," constantly challenge the success of habits. Those who are comfortable and complacent must find an environment conducive to accepting their habitual lifestyle. Possible, but not probable. The alternative is to become so confident in your habits that you can massage and modify them to facilitate performance in a changing environment. These are exciting people, committed to perceptual behavior. Risk-takers are those who thrive on stress. These people live on the emotional edge.

Perceptual people use anxiety as an asset as opposed to a liability in performing the tasks at hand. It seems that in reviewing the normal life cycle, there are at least two deterrents to perceptual development. Several research studies a few years ago, indicate that infants who were sedentary seemed to learn more quickly than those who were active. If this is true, I would suspect that long-term followup research would indicate that those children who were very active would be better able to apply their knowledge than the more sedentary youngsters. Knowledge without application and development of habits through observation inhibit perceptual development. Exploring one's environment in combination with knowledge, facilitates learning of life skills, enabling one to become more perceptual. When basic habits are not successful, perceptual children are able to modify habits to be successful in different environments. When I have an opportunity to address teachers, I encourage them to use their expertise, whether it's math, science, art, music, and so forth, to teach children life skills. These skills enable them to get closer to their potential in an every changing world and to recover more quickly from unexpected adversity.

Another potential detriment to perceptual development is technology. Technology may be our greatest asset, but it may also become a liability to our development. Education has become more efficient while losing its effectiveness. Too many children are spending more time on their computers and less time being active with their environment. They skip learning basic skills which might lead to perceptual behaviors and instead depend on technology to provide them with everything they need. In some universities, students are required to have a laptop computer enabling them to not attend classes. Lecture notes are provided on the computer. This mode of education is very similar to home schooling, which is a social development tragedy for children. The home school athletes with whom I work are lacking in life skills, skills needed to live in the real world. A large percentage of these students are efficient, they are intelligent, but are not prepared to use their knowledge in a perceptual way. Technology would be more beneficial to young people if it was a part of the educational process, not the total educational process.

The transition from habitual to perceptual behaviors is very clearly observed in sports, making sport participation, at any level, a valuable experience. Basic habits get athletes to a certain level of success, but the most successful athletes are able to expand habits into perceptual movements. These movements depend on several factors in the competitive environment, including opponent's talent and their perception of what it takes to win. One of my clients is a world-class professional tennis player. He serves in excess of 135 mph and he supplements that serve with exceptional basic skills, which become perceptual skills. If he was not able to change his game within a match, he would be okay; but not exceptional. Another client is a great baseball pitcher. By learning to modify his pitches during a game, he has progressed from being a good pitcher to a great pitcher who holds several season and post-season records. I personally witnessed him change his grip or his arm movement in the middle of a game to be more effective in that particular game. He will be in the Baseball Hall of Fame, because he is the consummate perceptual pitcher. A few years ago, a major league baseball team with whom I worked, signed a college player who was acknowledged to be one of the best hitters in the college ranks at that time. He had tremendous basic skills and a beautiful swing. When he reached the major league level, he found that his basic swing was not enough. He could not adjust his swing to hit against the major league pitchers. His explanation was that his basic swing had been good enough through his high school and college years. When he had to become perceptual, his career was over. One reason that less than 2% of the players signed by professional teams make it to the major leagues is that they have great basic skills, but are unable or unwilling to become perceptual in the performance. Other present and former high profile athletes such as Pete Maravich, Michael Jordon, Kobie Bryant, and Lebron James, to name a few NBA players, and Peyton Manning, Tom Brady, and Brett Farve in the NFL, are examples of exceptionally perceptual athletes.

Obviously, basic talent is pre-requisite to being successful. But equally obvious is that talent plus the ability to be perceptual, takes you to another level. The corporate environment also offers daily opportunities to become perceptually successful. As previously mentioned, I have attended sales meetings where participants are encouraged and even directed to get back to your habits. This position is troubling because it's not followed by comments relating to using those habits to move toward perceptual behaviors. As previously mentioned, bookstore shelves are packed with books promoting the magical power of habits. No doubt, people with solid habits perform at a relatively successful level and are usually very efficient. However, efficiency may not be the answer to long-term success. In past years, a few companies stood above the rest, simply because their products were the best. This has changed drastically. Like it or not, to stay in the market place, everybody has to be good. The quality across companies is basically the same. The critical question in the corporate world today is "if everyone has equal products, what separates us from the rest?" The answer is simple. Efficiency is not good enough. You must also be effective. More companies are emphasizing development of relationships. Customers are buying from people they like and trust. People who can break from basic habits and help them solve problems. This changing dynamic makes it critical that corporate employees and management become more perceptual regarding coworkers and clients. Poor communication skills are the fertilizer for conflict. Good communication skills are the perceptual skills that breed winners. It also seems that corporate people who are perceptual are happier with themselves than those who depend on habits.

A great environment to distinguish between perceptual

and habitual people is the airport, especially when there are flight delays. Habitual travelers are more likely to exhibit rage and complain to anyone who will listen, to attack the agent verbally, throw things down and use their cell phones to complain to friends who live thousands of miles away. So much wasted energy leads to an unhealthy lifestyle. The perceptual travelers, however, will read a book, strike up a conversation with a stranger, take a quick nap, find a space where their children can move around and explore, may plug in the computer to get some work done, or to play a game.

Another occupation which requires exceptional perception is parenting. As previously mentioned, parenting classes and books sell well but offer little practical knowledge. These books are popular because parents are searching for answers in response to the challenges kids face in and around the educational environment. Many of these books present solutions to generic issues, most of which do not exist in the real world. And most parents "parent" in the way they were parented. We coach the way we were coached. Today, however, kids are influenced more by peer groups than by parents. Decisions are much more difficult to make, resulting in more bad decisions. Parents have to be the most perceptual people in the world. It's a fine line to walk, instilling basic habits yet realizing that kids are going to be challenged daily. Consequently parents, like athletes and corporate employees, must help their children to become more perceptual, to weigh environmental factors and behave accordingly. Parents must also remember that kids are going to make bad decisions, which really enable them to learn how to recover more quickly and more effectively from adversity. Sometimes, the most valuable learning experiences come from adverse situations. These situations are critical teaching tools for parents.

The last group I want to discuss is a growing population in the world: senior citizens and those with chronic illnesses. The environment can be very frustrating for these people, primarily because they often are no longer able to execute their life-long habits. For example, I have Multiple Sclerosis. MS is a very frustrating and devastating disease with a suicide rate over seven times the national average. It is a disease for which there is no cure. Nothing needs the need to be perceptual to reality more than having habits taken away. You have to be more perceptive of the surfaces on which you walk, more aware of how you spend your energy and more perceptive of landmarks when driving to prevent getting lost. Multi-tasking is a thing of the past and planning ahead for events and vacations is very difficult. I have been living with MS for more than seven years and am learning every day how to be more perceptive and creative to ensure that life is fun every day. There are too many symptoms to list here, but suffice it to say that life for folks with chronic illnesses is a daily challenge. Age alone presents challenges to senior citizens. We cannot do many of the things we used to do. We must become more perceptive every day. Regardless of how many habits are taken away, the one trait that we all maintain control over is our attitude. There are no guarantees in life, but a positive attitude keeps the probability of success on your side.

FINAL THOUGHTS

In reviewing ideas presented in previous chapters, it seems that becoming perceptual is a natural consequence of life-long learning experiences. Not true! The natural consequence is to be a very good habitual person. The critical challenge is to use this foundation to become a risk-taking, stress seeking person who accepts every day and every situation (and welcomes stress) as an opportunity to increase his/her volume of perceptual growth. What separates great race drivers from good drivers, great hitters from good hitters, great executives from good executives, head coaches from assistant coaches, happy people from sad people, productive people with chronic illnesses from sad surviving people with chronic illness, is that great, productive, happy people look forward to every day in order to flaunt their perceptual behaviors and to break away from habitual behaviors.

The more perceptual you become, the more successful you become in all areas of your life. The better equipped mentally you become the quicker you recover from adversity. The more perceptual you become, the more you are able to recognize the valuable perceptual behaviors in other people. The more perceptual you become, the more you recognize that the process of achieving goals must be fluid. The more perceptual you become, the more you learn how to surround yourself with people who support your emotional traits and who help you massage habits. To become perceptual is an obvious challenge and will very often be uncomfortable. But achieving success in your life should include adversity along the way. When you become frustrated or anxious during certain situations, just remember that there are very few guarantees in life. Perhaps the only guarantee made in this chapter is that people with a solid foundation of talent, who have learned how to use that talent in a perceptive way and who have positive expectations every day, will always have a high probability of success. In real life, you cannot do anything you want, but by becoming more perceptual in your behavior, you can do more than you are doing today.

CONDITIONED HABITS

1. _____

2. _____

3. _____

4. _____

5. _____

PERCEPTUAL PLAN
(ALTERNATIVES TO HABITS)

1. _____

2. _____

3. _____

4. _____

5. _____

CHAPTER 6

Practice the Mechanics of Quick Recovery

We have spent the first five chapters talking about the things you need to have in place in order for you to be able to recover from adversity. We've talked about identifying assets and liabilities, making a plan, surrounding yourself with the right people, having positive expectations, and then really being able to stick to your plan once you've established where you want to go. We've talked about identifying "the mud in the water"—sifting through the things in your mind to decide what to keep, what to eliminate, and what to categorize in your mind. Now we move to the process of recovering.

The mechanics of recovering from adversity will enable you to recover much quicker than you ever have before. You see, the issue is not necessarily being able to recover from adversity. The issue is how quickly you can recover.

If I'm dealing with a pitcher in baseball, can he recover from a bad pitch within five seconds to make the next pitch, or does he require 15 to 20 minutes to recover from the bad pitch just before the next inning? It's obvious that it's advantageous to recover in five seconds. With a hitter in baseball, does he recover between swings or does he recover between the bats? Even though the answers to these questions are obvious, the behaviors are not always obvious. It's a process that everyone has to go through in order to recover more quickly.

The number one thing that we have to keep in mind is that in order to recover from adversity and recover quickly, you have to realize to which level you are aiming to recover—where do you want to go. You want to avoid recovering *from* adversity and pursue recovering *to* success. In other words, if a baseball pitcher throws a bad pitch and during the next pitch his mind is dwelling on the pitch before with the aim of *not* throwing another bad pitch, then basically he has no chance to throw a good pitch. In his mind, the bad pitch is now behind and in front of him. If you focus on avoiding a bad swing and only hope a good swing will happen, you basically have no chance for a good swing. The same thing holds true for salespeople. If you leave a bad sales meeting and hope to not have another bad sales meeting, then you really have very little chance of success. If you have a chronic illness such as MS, and you fall, the worst thing you can think about when you stand up is that you don't want to fall again, because you probably will fall again. You don't get up from a fall to not fall again. You get up from a fall to walk. It's a state of mind. You have to put the probability of recovering quickly on your side. Time is not your friend when you talk about recovering from adversity. The mechanics are relatively simple and not that difficult to execute if you are committed. You have to be committed to recovery. One of the comments that I make to groups of MS patients is that it easy to feel bad and it's difficult to feel good. But once you've gone through the process of trying to recover to feeling good, then you have crossed a hurdle and you feel better than you ever imagined you could feel and it will be easier the next time you feel bad to pursue feeling good. I have been in that position and I know that it is human nature to just accept feeling bad and focus only on getting through the day. But you can't be willing to settle for feeling bad every day. Once you give the day away, you can never get it back. How you view the process of recovery is all-important here. As I said previously, you're not recovering *from* something; you are recovering *to* good performance. That performance may be walking, playing a sport, having a good meeting, or whatever goal you may set for yourself, just remember you're recovering *to* something good. Never run away from adversity, but rather always move forward towards something good and positive.

When something negative happens, back off mentally. Take a moment and "see" yourself performing the skill, or the task, or engaging in the activity correctly. We'll talk about visualization as an important process in recovery later in this chapter. If it's a conversation that did not go well, then immediately take a few minutes to yourself and replay the conversation. Don't wait! Don't wait until you get home; don't wait until it's a convenient time; do it immediately following the activity. Determine what went well and what could have gone better. You can't accurately make that analysis if you wait a period of time. Determine how it will be better the next time. Then the next time you're performing well or engaging in the skill, there will be little if any adversity because you've made the corrections beforehand. So in a sense, it helps you stay away from the reactive process which may be riddled with errors, and gives you a much better feeling of preparation. Videotaping is a common tool used to correct performance. It allows people to watch their performance and then visualize an improved performance. If you don't have videotape available to you, then you will have to form a picture in your mind of what is correct and what's successful. For example, it may be a speech to a group that you haven't spoken with before. If you spend time before the meeting getting to know people, getting a feel for the mood in the room, walking through the room, testing the microphone, going out into the seating area and looking back up to the stage – getting a feel for what the environment is going to be like when you speak, you're better able to curtail any adverse feelings that might occur when you actually begin the speech, and you eliminate the need to recover. If you have spoken before, visualize past successful performances. If you wake up in the morning and you're not walking well, but you walked well yesterday, then think back on yesterday and see yourself walking well. You repeat it over and over and over again. By mentally visualizing successful performance, you achieve faster recovery from any negative impact of the adversity, which in this case is being unable to walk well.

Think about how adversity "tastes." It tastes bad, it looks bad, it feels bad, and you don't want that taste or look or feel of the negative effects of adversity. Now you know, the quickest relief from that bad taste is what you have stored mentally. Realize that everything you have ever done, you have stored somewhere. I don't know that we understand exactly how people store information or how they arrange it when they store it, but the fact remains that we store everything we do. The good and the bad. There's something in your mind that you have done well and you can pull up that image of success. This skill will enable you to recover more quickly

Now let's consider how you recover quickly. How do you learn the process? The first step in the process is to accept that that adversity is real. It's a daily experience in life in most environments. Whether you are an athlete or a person walking around the streets, parent, professional person, a person walking around with chronic illness, with physical disabilities. Adversity is a part of your life.

Next, you have to assume that you will be better for having gone through the adversity process and the recovery process. There's a real issue with creating an error-free environment for young people. Because in an error-free environment, young people never have to learn to recover. I have had experiences with athletes who have been tremendous athletes growing up. One athlete, in particular, was a first-team all American high school football player and a first-team all American high school baseball player. He had scholarships to big university in football and he chose to sign a professional baseball contract. Well, his first three years in the minor league with his baseball team, he progressed through the process very quickly. He was successful at every level. He was called to the major leagues on a relatively fast tract. Realize here that of all players who sign professional contracts, less than 2 in 100 make it to the major leagues—this was an exceptional person and an exceptional athlete. He made it to the major leagues, his

third or fourth year, and he had a tremendous first year, leading the major leagues in two or three different hitting categories and at least one defensive category. He was playing in his
home town and was really riding the wave of success, which
he had done since he had started playing sports, probably at
the age of five or six. He had never really experienced failure,
had always been gifted athletically and had always been successful, very popular, very easy to be around. He was the kind
of person that our society would call the "full package." In his
second year in the major leagues, he went through a period of
hitting where he was experiencing incredible difficulty. He had
one stretch where he was five hits for 55 at bats—a very, very
serious hitting slump. He called and asked me to spend some
time with him. When I sat down with him, I just calmly sat
and stared. He asked me what I was doing. I said, "I'm looking
in your recovery bag for tools to recover from adversity and
your bag's empty. You've never had adversity before." If we
grow up as physical beings, we assume that physical talent will
take us to the ends of the earth. All of a sudden, we're confronted with competitors who are as physically talented as we
are and we suddenly find ourselves struggling to be successful
in this new environment of adversity. It's critical that children
be allowed to experience and handle adversity while they are
growing up in order to develop the tools to recover from it.
This proved a very tough thing to teach this particular athlete.
There comes a point where we need to supplement our physical talent with mental development. We need to add the skill
of recovering mentally from adversity as a part of that total
package. So, basically, what we had to do was go back and
learn this skill—to fill his tool bag full of tools to recover from

adversity, tools which would have been better acquired at the ages of 12, 13 or 14 years. It was fortunate that this person was able to do that and is now a very successful professional athlete—and an even better person all around.

But that doesn't always happen. I've seen careers in all areas—not just in the sports arena—which are needlessly wasted because the folks involved in those careers never learn to recover from adversity. It would seem that it is easier when confronted with adversity to run to the nearest exit—away from adversity in order to avoid dealing with it. You can try going to a new and fresh environment, free of adversity. Before long, life finds you again and presents you with a different version of that adversity. You may have found yourself some different circumstances and different adversities, but it's adversity nonetheless. In order to stop the frantic running, you need to learn the mechanics of recovery using everything that you have learned up through these first five chapters.

You may one of the lucky ones who have had experiences with adversity all through your life and learned to recover from adversity. You may feel you have plenty of tools to deal with adversity. Then all of a sudden, you are confronted with something that was completely unexpected. Maybe it is a disability from an accident, maybe it is a chronic disease (as in my case with MS), whatever it may be, you suddenly find the tools that were once sufficient are now not enough. I've always had a relatively easy time recovering from adversity because I developed the habit of looking ahead to the bright side. But when MS came into my life, it was devastating. I didn't have the tools in my recovery bag to deal with MS, because it was never expected and larger than anything I had faced before. It took a while to learn how to recover emotionally and mentally from the adversity and shock of learning that I have this devastating disease for which there is no cure. This is a point in your life when recovery takes a new direction. You have to go back and review your assets. Obviously, you now do not have as many assets as you had before. You can still emphasize all the remaining assets you do have. Just because your assets and liabilities have changed, physically and mentally in some areas, it doesn't mean that you need to fold your tent. It doesn't mean that you need to quit. The recovery process then becomes realizing that you need to flaunt your assets more than ever before in order to feel good about who you are and what you bring to the party every day. It's life as it is. You must realize that you are the same unique person you've always been and you still possess a mix of assets and liabilities. At this point, mentally recovering from a devastating adversity becomes possible and much easier.

So the first step in the mechanics of recovery from such a devastating blow is to accept that adversity is part of life. At times, it's expected and you may be able to nip it in the bud; at other times, it's unexpected and much more catastrophic, but you still need to make an effort to recover. You need to try to avoid the dark tunnels in your life that are filled with past mistakes and regrets. One of the worse habits of people is that they spend most of their lives looking at mistakes they've made and replaying them over and over. They then try to live their lives avoiding the any risk of making those same mistakes. The problem with this plan is you become unable to move on and you merely survive. You can never become successful at anything. If you want to look at the mistakes a time or two to learn how to correct them, that's fine. But then dispense with those; eliminate those thoughts. Dwelling on mistakes is like drinking poison every day – the negativity builds over time and chokes out life. The result is that people who handle adversity with this method are never able recover to a higher level of success. With images of past regrets and mistakes muddying up the water, they may actually forget there is always a higher level to grow towards. You just recover to the level of merely surviving and you learn to feel good about where you are. To me that is a superficial way to live your life.

Think about how long it takes you to recover from an adverse situation. How long do you carry the baggage around? If you're in sales and you make a presentation at 9 and get kicked out of the office at 9:05, how long is it before you're back to being yourself? Is it an hour, three hours, four hours? When it should be no more than 5 minutes to recover. If you think about how long it takes you to get upset, it's a matter of seconds, as opposed to the amount of time it takes to recover, which can be several hours sometimes. It shouldn't take any longer to recover than it does to get upset.

Basically, you cannot recover until you learn to recognize adversity, until you learn to recognize what winning really is in your life or being successful is in your life, until you learn some other mechanics that we'll discuss. But most of all, you have to be able recognize the assets that are going to enable you to recover from your list of assets that you listed in Chapter 2. You need to use those assets every day to help you recover. And you need to be able to get the "mud out of the water." You need to try to clear your mind of those things that are not important in the recovery process. For example, there may be things that are in your mind that you think about every day that you want to keep, that you want to hold onto, a death of a loved one, a relationship gone bad, or a relationship from the past. There may be any number of things that you want to remember, but you have to be able to categorize those things. You have to be able to take those good things you want to remember and have a "chest of drawers" or a "cabinet" where you can put those thoughts in the cabinet until you have time to think about them. That gives you more clear space in your mind. There are certain things that you have no control over, that you are thinking about every day. You can eliminate those things from your mind or give those issues to other people around you or on your team and let them deal with those issues, so that you clear more space in your mind so that you have more energy to recover. You're never going to have a completely clear mind. That process is not going to happen. But the more energy you can save and get back on the side of recovery, as opposed to using it for no worthwhile purpose, the more quickly and better able you are to recover. So once you've gotten the mud out of the water, now, you need to define what winning is. In other words, in your life, what's successful? What means to you that you have recovered from adversity? What would you be able to do that would indicate you had recovered. If you could not walk five steps one day and the next day you were walking around the house or walking to the mailbox, would that indicate to you that you had recovered from that adversity? Now, this is each individual's decision to make. Second, it's essential that you learn to recognize the signs of adversity. In other words, there is a tendency on the part of people to ignore the signs of adversity and just assume that it doesn't exist. This can result in a worst case scenario which would require much more time to recover than if you had acted quickly when you encountered the problems or the mistakes or the failures, whatever the adversity might be. It doesn't always hit you in the face and there are subtle signs sometimes that adversity is occurring, and the signs are different for everyone. There are no magic answers. There is no list to follow. But you can learn to recognize when things are not as they should be. You may feel tension, you may become unsure of yourself, you may become tentative about a presentation. You may become more anxious during some performance or presentation. If any of those things happen, then it may be a sign that adversity is beginning to creep into your system. By recognizing that it's there, you can then take action. Third, you really need to learn to visualize. Visualize correct performance. See yourself in an environment performing well. If I'm going to walk a half mile tomorrow at a national park, I sit before and I visualize and I mentally see myself walking a half mile in the park. It's not that hard to do and everybody can do that. So learning to visualize really facilitates better focus, which is essential in recovery. Focusing enables you to develop a plan to pursue success and to recover. So visualization is an important tool for you to be able to use. I had a coach one time tell me that true visualization was seeing yourself in color. In other words, seeing every part of everything in the environment is the true visualization process. The next step is to have selective attention. In other words, when we receive information into our system, we received that information from many different sources. You feel it, you touch it, you see it, you hear it, you smell it. Once you receive all that information and it gets to the colander in your mind where the good information is sifted from the bad, retaining the good and allowing the bad to flow out. In other words, what is important? What are the important things that you need to achieve in catching a baseball? Well, it involves tremendous selective attention. You see the person's arm come forward, release the ball and then you catch the ball. Now if you've never caught a ball, then you'll probably see the trees behind the person throwing it, you'll see the cars, you'll see the dogs, you'll hear the birds. All these worthless cues are in your system, because you haven't learned how to have selective attention for that particular skill. So once you get the selective attention, then, "Oh, I'm going to catch a baseball," plug in the cues that are needed and catch the ball. It sounds simple, but the same process in necessary in dealing with adversity. What is the adversity, what are the things I need in my system to be able to recover, how can I use my assets and how can I process this information together to achieve a positive outcome? Selective attention is very critical. In some environments, it is very interesting that when you learn to recover from adversity, you're going to encounter people who don't seem to be your friends anymore because you are doing things they cannot do because you are learning to recover. You are accomplishing things that they maybe would like to do but are not willing to put in the time to do. You need to understand that these people are superficial friends and they are not your friends anyway. A cold thing to say, but true. You need to understand that you need to take care of you. And the better you take care of yourself, then the more quality energy you're going to have for other people. So the quicker you recover from adversity, the more energy you have saved, the more quality energy that you can give to other people. You need to also understand that your success in recovery really affects other people during the recovery process. Other people on your team, if you'll look back in the book to the chapter on surrounding yourself with the right players your team members may be involved with your recover. They need to know what the cues to recover are. You need to talk with your team members about where you are trying to recover to and what you're trying to accomplish. You need to involve your team in the recovery process.

And finally, recovery takes patience. You need to learn to be patient. You may take one forward step forward and two back; and then one step forward and one back; and then one step and then two steps forward; and then the process will lead you in the right direction. Don't spend too much time looking at the end result and make sure that the process of recovery is on track. When I say patient, I'm not talking about days or weeks or months. I believe being patient comes every few minutes, it may be an hour, it may be two hours. But you have to let the process lead you toward recovery. Very simply said, I believe we need to be patient, yet persistence.

I'll end this chapter with a true short story. I had an athlete a few years ago who was a professional baseball player. He was a tremendous hitter with incredible power. He had gone through a stretch of probably a month where he hadn't really shown any of this power. He was very frustrated and in a deep slump. We sat down together and I asked him, "Can you remember one time, the last time, when you hit a ball hard and it was like music? It was just vintage you?" He sat for a moment, and then his eyes began to tear up. He got excited and sat up on the edge of his seat, and said, "Yeah, I do! It was a Tuesday night, three weeks ago. The temperature was kind of cool. It was late in the game and we were behind 2 to 1; the count was three balls and one strike on me, in the seventh inning. I hit a ball that was really vintage me. I hit a home run and we won." My next question was, "When was the last time you thought about that hit?" His answer, which I expected, was, "probably not since that night." The reason for telling this story is pretty simple. As I've said before, we remember everything we've done and we store everything we've done. Because of the way our society operates, we are always reminded of negative things which make it difficult to recover. We have to make a conscious effort to realize there are two files in our minds: one is filled with negative things and one has positive things that we've done. And that hit has always been there since he did it, but he never chose to use it to recover. Pull out the good things that you've done many times to help you recover. Things that may not even be related to what you're trying to recover from at this point, but at least they give you a positive mind set so that you can expect something good to happen and increase the probably that you'll recover from the adversity. When I have adversity, I think about this story often, because I'll never forget the look on his face when he began to talk about the vintage performance. To have realized that it had always been there and he had just not used it was really reward to see. He began to recover more quickly and he got his power back within a few games, and life went on. You can look back in your life, you will find a lot of these things that will really help you develop the right mind set to recover, not only to get the mud out of the water and to recover, but to recover more quickly. The key is not recovery—the key is quick recovery.

ADVERSITY
(MUD IN THE WATER)

1. _____

2. _____

3. _____

4. _____

5. _____

RECOVERY PLAN

1. _____

2. _____

3. _____

4. _____

5. _____

CHAPTER 7

Challenging Stress and Adversity Makes You Better

Stress is unquestionably a determining factor in succeeding versus surviving. Stress is a factor in everything you do every day, both professionally and personally. Winners thrive on stress. These are folks who I categorize as stress-seekers. Survivors, on the other hand, expend enormous amounts of energy avoiding stressors. Consequently, they only survive at best. The people who I have dealt with over the past 40 years in sports and in the corporate environment, as well as in other environments, and particularly those who have chronic illnesses, realize that stress is always there. Stress is, initially at least, perceived as negative by almost everyone. But we need to understand that stress, or the severity of the stress, is not what makes us sick and causes various negative things in our lives. It is how we perceive and react to that stress. This will be surprising to you if you've always been told that stress is an entirely, and even overwhelming, negative influence in your life.

How much time do you spend each day trying to rid your life of stress? How much does stress cause industry every year? Billons of dollars are spent by corporations in dealing with stress. Much of that cost is in disability payments. Employees can retire from some professions after seven years with as much as 75% disability caused by job related stress. It would seem that stress is a significantly negative factor in terms of productivity and health. However, probably more than 80% of stress factors are neither positive nor negative when they confront your system. Stressors become negative primarily because of perception. We hear the word stress and immediately begin thinking of all the things that are wrong with our lives. We seldom think of the positive aspects that actually act as motivators to make positive changes that will improve our lives. Stress management seminars are very popular as a way of teaching people how to relax and eliminate stress. But too often, these seminars are nothing more than knee-jerk reactions to a traditional definition of stress. The truth is that your mindset causes most stressors to become negative.

Of course, I'm referring mostly to those stressors that cause you mental anguish. There are obviously physical stressors that are extremely negative, at least initially, to those who suffer from disabilities, those who have had accidents, and those who have chronic illnesses. Even in those instances, there are enough assets available to you, already present within your system, so that your life can continue to be very productive—if you use the stressors as incentives (motivators) to accomplish things.

By definition, stress is the amount of wear and tear on the body. It has a physiological impact on the body. For instance, stressors are with you when you walk causing stress on the joints in your legs. When you throw, you have stress on your arms and shoulders. When you talk, there is stress on your vocal cords. Even when you breathe, there is stress on your respiratory system. Another physiological example is the fight or flight response. So there are physical stressors everywhere, every day, in everyone's life. You need to accept the fact that this is true and will probably always be true. When you fail to accept these physical and physiological stressors as normal, they can develop into psychological issues.

There is also psychological noise in the environment that can cause stress or distress. Things like crowd noises at sports and horns blowing in traffic, and even colors of clothing, wall colors, and pictures in offices, are all considered psychological noise. As a matter of fact, many years ago, there were some researches who published the famous Hawthorne studies in which the researchers painted the walls of the secretaries' offices over the weekend without mentioning it to the secretaries. When they returned to work on Monday, their productivity increased significantly. They placed pictures of favorite scenes on the walls and their productivity increased even more. The researchers went into production facilities and changed the lighting levels on the production lines. When they turned the lighting up to above normal, productivity went up. Then they turned the lighting down below normal and productivity went up. They turned the lighting back to the normal level and productivity went up again. The workers perceived the changes in their work environment as evidence that company officials cared about them.

There are many ways to deal with stress, but the first thing we have to realize is that stressors are not necessarily meant to shut your system down. Many times, in fact, most times they are meant to be incentives to enable you to become better. Stressors make you what you are and drive you to be where you need to be. They can drive you to the emotional edge, get you where you need to be in emotional arousal in order to obtain that optimum level of performance. If they don't drive you to become better, stressors may make you worse through illness, such as depression or burnout. Stressors can drive you to fail. Success or failure depends on your perception of the stressors. The operative term is "perception." Because of conditioning, both personally and professionally, people tend to panic when under great stress. They let stress take control of their lives. This happens often with young people. It is not an issue for only the older or the middle aged person. This is an issue for everyone. I've known parents whose 5 year-old kindergartners were in counseling due to stress in their environment. I've known people no older than 26 who have had heart attacks related to stress. Stress really does not discriminate. It affects everyone. In the work place, stress related problems cause such wide-spread symptoms as headaches, nervous tension, irritability, complaints of burnout, wasted time and poor time management, all contribute in some respects to absentism which was a major issue for business, especially in the present economic environment.

To repeat, up to 80% of stress is neither positive nor negative. Traffic is an obvious example of something that stresses, yet isn't inherently negative. Other stressors are deadlines, financial resources or lack of, and lack of other resources. People are stressors. Children are stressors. Bills are stressor.

Almost everything you can imagine that affects your life creates some degree of stress. All these stressors can become assets to your productivity, or they can become detrimental. Every day we have stressors that will be put into either the incentive/positive shelf, or the detriment/negative shelf. Choose to put those stressors, if at all possible, on the positive side of life. The key is how you deal with stress. That is a serious and conscious choice that every person has to make for themselves. At one point in my life, I was partially paralyzed. I was in the Mayo Clinic in Rochester, Minnesota. The diagnosis was a stress-related condition for which I had to be hospitalized for an extended period of time. Though I've never been sure if stress was the problem, or if the diagnosis of stress was simply a convenient diagnosis, nonetheless I recovered and began to do probably ten times as much as I did before. My productivity soared because I learned to take better care of myself. I exercised more, and I ate better. I looked at things from a different perspective. Since then, I've never been happier personally or professional despite the many stressors since that time. In 2004, I was diagnosed with Multiple Sclerosis. People with chronic illness understand that stress is a major issue with these illnesses, and I was definitely under stress. I had no idea what it MS was and I had no idea how devastating it could be. The only thing I knew was that it was not good. So after having spent many days and nights wondering and worrying about what was going to happen to me and really feeling sorry for myself, I came to realize that there was a purpose for all of this. I acknowledged that it was indeed a stressor, but I could use it to become better a person. I had probably gotten complacent in my profession. I believed my programs were still good, but I'm not so sure that I appreciated them as much as I should have. I began to work harder, I began to have more control over my time and really became, I think, more productive than before I was diagnosed. I certainly learned to appreciate every day of my life more than I had before. With that in mind, I made a conscious choice to turn that stress into a positive incentive in my life and have never looked back. Obviously, not everyone is able to do that, but at least everyone has the capability emotionally to take control of their lives under stress and to be able to salvage some good things out of it to make themselves better and to be happy.

There are many typical reactions to stress. We will discuss four or five of those. There are also ways to recognize stress and ways to deal with it in a positive way and we will discuss those also. The important note here is that when you have many, many things on your mind that you are thinking about, worrying about or trying to attend to, you are going to have undue stress in your life. You may try to give everything equal consideration and equal time and hope for positive results in every situation and that's probably not going to be the case. You have to begin to prioritize. We have talked about this in several previous chapters that you need to be able to sit down and list the things that are on your mind and prioritize and eliminate. You will need to give your emotional attention to those that are most important at this time. There are many stressful situations that people go through in which they become physically disabled. Well, if you are physically disabled, you are still the same person you've always been; you have just been given new stress now, and will have to figure out new ways to do the same things. It can be done. It is a choice that you need to make. If you have a chronic illness or if you have memory issues, as in my case, the absence of short-term memory, you may have to write more things down. You have to learn to enjoy every single day. You don't set long-term extensive goals. You set goals every day and in some cases, you set goals hourly. What those goals do is help you deal with stress. If you have something specific that you're trying to do as opposed to letting the stress in your life cause you to put things off or procrastinate, then having goals is going to help you to get the job done. You will feel better having accomplished some things on your list. As I've said several times in this book, it's easy to feel bad and hard to feel good. But once you do the things that are necessary to feel good, like using stress as an incentive, it is amazing how much more productive you can be.

There are a lot of stress reactions. They are generally categorized into five different areas. I don't think any of those five are particularly helpful to you, but they are typical ways that people deal with stress and you need to know about them.

Withdrawal. In other words, removing yourself from a stressful environment. I think sometimes strategic withdrawal is okay if you need time to get your ideas together and to think about things before you confront stress. But just withdrawing from stress in order to avoid emotional exposure to stress or confronting stress can be detrimental to your system, because when you come back to the environment, most likely the stress is still there and will probably be even more significant than before.

Helplessness. I think everyone at some point in their lives

have probably experienced this feeling, especially when you're sitting in traffic, or when you having a bad day and you feel bad, you are ill and medication doesn't seem to be helping. A feeling of helplessness can creep into your system very, very quickly. It inhibits recovery and can really shut your system down. So you need to do whatever you can to avoid a feeling of helplessness. I think it's going to happen, but when I say avoid, I guess I'm talking about recovering from it as quickly as possible. If you have a feeling of helplessness in a stressful environment, then try to mentally think of some situations you've been in which caused maybe the same feeling and think about what you did to recover from that feeling before. At least it will give you a springboard for recovery in this instance.

Internalizing. I believe this one may be potentially the most hazardous to your health, because the more you hold stressors in, then the more apt you are to have problems with headaches and ulcers and rashes and all kinds of physical issues as a result of keeping stress in, not talking about it, not dealing with it, and not letting people on your team help you deal with it. Internalizing is a very scary way to deal with stress. Stress doesn't get any better by holding it inside.

Over-control. Many people in stressful environments tend to over-control those around them. If it's in a corporate environment, they tend to become micro-managers and subsequently they lose a lot of good employees because of their micro-managing because they are over-controlling. At least one example of a situation that I can recall in sports, where the general manager was incredible over-controlling. Because of that, no one really was permitted to do their job without answering to this person. My feeling has always been, you hire good people and you let them work. It's like in sports, the managers job is to have good players and put them on the field and let them play. Over-managing is worse than no management at all. Lack of control (if you have good people) is a better environment than too much control. Because no one gets better in the environment. So over-control, at least for the long-term, is certainly not a viable way to deal with stress.

Emotional outburst. This is my favorite. It is the most interesting. I think a lot of people who have stress and who may have appeared before in situations to be pretty mild-mannered quite people and all of a sudden the stress that they have been internalizing has gotten to be too much for their system and they have an emotional outburst. Everybody has probably done this at one time or another—some people in front of other people, some people by themselves. But an emotional outburst of 30 seconds may cause you years of loyalty and respect from people around you. It may even cost you friendships.

You need to give a lot of thought to how you want to react to stress, at least emotionally. If you look at those five ways of dealing with stress, I think you would be hard-pressed to convince me that any of those five is the desirable route to take.

If I can add one thing to that list that I think would be positive, it would be number 6, to look forward to and thrive on stress. Stress will either make you great or in some cases, cause you to die. It's your choice to make. If you ask 100 people who are recovering from heart attacks brought on by stress and ask them how they feel, an overwhelming number will tell you

they feel better than they've felt in 20 years and are more productive. My question to you then would be very simple: Why
do we have to have a heart attack before we get healthy?

Based on over 40 years in dealing with professional athletes, corporations and many folks with chronic illness, I've
developed a few keys for thriving on stress. These keys may
at least give you an idea of how to pursue positive outcomes.
Remember that all stressors can be either potential assets or
liabilities. It's your choice to make. In fact, the most dangerous stressors seem to be the small picky things that come up
every day, not necessarily the major events. I think a lot of
people who have gone through catastrophic injuries and life
altering situations have gotten through those and are stronger
than they were before, at least emotionally. It's the little things
that pop up every day and you deal with them and they seem
to pop up the next day and the next day. Those are the stressors that you probably need to get in order and react to.

KEY 1: I think it's important that we separate the stressors
from the symptoms. We often reach with pretty significant
amounts of emotion to symptoms and never get to the
sources. If you will recall in Chapter 2, when we talked about
assets and liabilities, the comment was made that if there's a
list of ten liabilities and you really examine that list, then
you'll find that there may be two or three true liabilities and
the other seven or eight issues are really just symptoms of
those two or three stressors. So basically, if you list all the
things that cause stress in your life, then re-examine that list,
and I don't care if there's ten or twenty or fifty, examine that
list and try to identify the basic stressors, the basic issues and

then list the symptoms under those so that you're in a position then to deal with four or five stressors as opposed to a list of twenty or thirty. It will enable you to get off to a much more positive start.

KEY 2: Try to drain your emotion from stressful situations. The better you can drain the emotion out of conflicts and out of situations then the better off you are going to be. A way to do that is to list the elements of the stressor and then when emotions begins to run higher than is comfortable, you can always go back to the list. If you're going to have a situation that is going to be stressful to you, list the things you want to deal with before you go sit down to deal with it and then if the conversation becomes emotional, then you can always go back to the list you have because an emotional discussion of stressors just makes stress worse.

KEY 3: Take some time and list all your stressors, both personally and professionally. If you make a comprehensive list in no particular order, then you're going to be able to identify a lot of things that you may consider stressors that may even be incentives already in your life. In relationships for example, there are a lot of stressors in relationships that we need to deal with in order to make the relationship stronger. You can withdraw as we mentioned before on the list of ways to deal with stress, and that situation gets worse and can get to the point where there is no recovery. That's unacceptable.

KEY 4: Once you have your list of stressors, decide which stressors can be changed to assets. The best way to do this is to write an action for changing each stressor to an asset. In other words, sit down, look at the stressor and write an action: "What am I going to do to make this a productive element in my life?" Make the action specific. It's almost like setting goals, which we talked about in an earlier chapter. Make it specific, make it attainable and put a timeline on it. If you need help changing that stressor to an asset in your life or an incentive, then call on those folks who are on your team, which a concept that was also discussed in an earlier chapter. Surround yourself with the right people, those who will be honest with you and will ask you tough questions to help you deal with the stress.

Here is a very important suggestion for dealing with stress: Select a simple stressor that you are going to deal with and change into a positive incentive in your life. Initially, choose a stressor that will give you a feeling of accomplishment and fulfillment once you have dealt with it. In other words, start out with an easier stressor so that you can taste the feeling of accomplishment and perhaps self-fulfillment and you can move then to the more complicated and more cumbersome stressors. But deal with those you can nip in the bud and deal with in a very quick and efficient manner first.

I'm sure you have heard over the years that it is a good practice to talk to yourself sometimes, and I don't think that is a bad idea. I think the last suggestion I have for you in dealing with stress is to verbalize to yourself that you are better after having dealt with a stressor than you were before you started. You need to encourage yourself, especially if there are not others around to encourage you to give you a sense of accomplishment. Now remember, if you play to accomplish something every day, which you should, then you must thrive on stress. I'll never forget, many years ago, John Smoltz, a pitcher for the Atlanta Braves, who still may be the best big game pitcher in baseball because he always thrived on the challenge and the stress of big games. He held the record for many years for play-off game victories. Why? Because those were the games with the most stress and consequently the games he most looked forward to.

Again, we review what I consider to be the very foundation for achievement and quick recovery from adversity and quick recovery in stressful environments. That is simply having positive expectations. You need to know what you expect of yourself and others in stressful environments. Let others know what you expect of them. It's a major step toward reducing stress in the environment. A large percentage of people leave jobs every day, not because they don't like the job, the job environment or the pay, it's because they don't fully know what's expected of them. They are told to work hard and do their job, which basically says nothing. Without specific expectations, frustration, doubt and confusion may cause a very stressful situation leading to activation of the fight or flight syndrome. In most cases, people will chose to leave the environment.

Another suggestion I would have is to try to exercise as much as you can whenever you can. The value of exercise is far too vast to discuss in this chapter, but exercise is critical in dealing with stress. It also gives you, in most cases, time alone to think things through without the clutter that is usually around in your personal and professional environments. Try to keep it fun. Stress can do any number of things to us and can also do any number of things for us, if we try to keep it fun. You can find the fun side of anything if you take time to do it. I've had some interesting situations recently that caused me to either be very frustrated or to laugh it off and have fun. With Multiple Sclerosis, one of the issues is balance. I fell recently while walking on a city square and tumbled out into the street, breaking a couple of ribs. I have long hair and I'm lying in the street and people are just passing by waving at me and I'm waving back. I called my son to come get me. He and I then sat on the sidewalk laughing about what had happened, because people were just waving at me. His response was, "Dad, they just thought you were homeless and were sleeping on the sidewalk." My response was "if they had stopped, I would have asked them for money, because I knew some of those people." It was a situation that could have been very frustrating and could have led to a lot of stress. Instead, I was able to perceive the situation as being somewhat funny. It took me a few weeks to get over the physical problems, but I had recovered from the emotional shock by the time I got up and sat on the curb. You have to accept the fact that stress is a part of your life and in many ways stressors can put some levity in your daily life. When it's all said and done, every day should be basically an exciting day for you!

STRESSORS

1. _____

2. _____

3. _____

4. _____

5. _____

ACTION PLAN TO USE
OR ELIMINATE STRESSORS

1. _____

2. _____

3. _____

4. _____

5. _____

CHAPTER 8

Stretch Your Emotions Every Day

This is without question the most fun chapter, at least for me. I've spent the last 39 years working with emotional aspects of performance, both in the corporate environment and in sports. Over the past seven years, I've dedicated my time to working with MS patients to try to enable them to get back in touch with their emotions. We need to understand that emotions basically make us who we are. We all have physical characteristics and talents, but emotions dictate how we perform, communicate and interact with others. They dictate how we socialize. Emotions can be tremendous assets, but they can also be detrimental to performance if they are not controlled. So that being said, it's critical that any time you begin to perform whatever task it might be, it's important that you be emotionally under control. In other words, one of the worst things that can happen is for a person to be completely relaxed when they are trying to perform a task. Various levels of emotion are required to supplement performance in every task, based on the task complexity. For simpler tasks such as walking and running, gross motor skills, then emotion doesn't have to be as high and probably should be a bit lower than average, but can still be a supplement to the execution of those skills. As the skill becomes more complex, then emotions need to rise higher until the complexity reaches a certain point where emotions need to be lower. In other words, there is an optimal level of emotion for top performance in every single task. An important rule of thumb to remember is that the more complex the task, the lower the emotion can be to be effective. The simpler that the task becomes, then emotion can be higher. In sports, a good example would be a defensive lineman who reacts in performance. If reaction is the key, then the anxiety or emotional level can be much higher. When you deal with what they call skill positions in football such as quarterback, receiver, or a running back, then the emotional level will be at a lower level. If we look at emotion from one to ten, one being completely relaxed and ten being extremely emotional, probably somewhere around six to seven is the optimal level for emotion to be under control, and to be what we call in sports psychology "performing on the edge". Most people when they perform will perform lower than the emotional edge because they are uncomfortable being on the edge, realizing that being there means that if something goes wrong with performance, then frustration will drive them over the edge. Nobody likes to be over the edge which means you're basically out of control emotionally. One of the tasks that we have in dealing with emotions of athletes is that we have to put something in their "mental bag" so that if they go over the edge they can get back in a matter of seconds. It's interesting that in every sporting event you will see at some point emotions go over the edge and somebody does something that is against the rules. All that means is that they don't have the capacity emotionally to control their emotions. It's very critical that we understand emotional levels and understand that emotions is part of what we do, but the important factor here is that no matter what level your emotions might be, they need to be under control. So when a coach says to an athlete, just relax and play the game, what they're really saying is keeping your emotions under control. This is one of the phrases that are often misinterpreted by athletes. At the beginning of the professional major league baseball draft which takes place every June, we administer personality inventories to all the draft eligible athletes. That personality inventory has 21 basic personality traits plus 19 that we consider to be second order traits. Weights are given to each of the basic traits to come up with the second order traits. Of those personality traits, 11 of them deal directly with emotion. It's very important to realize when teams are looking at athletes they pay particular attention to the emotion they show in performance, and also how they control those emotions during performance. Before and after the performance is studied as well. There are different levels of emotion evident in those three situations. We have what we call a pre-performance anxiety level which is obviously an emotional level that is relatively high in most cases. Once the performance begins, we have the performance level. The pre-performance level drops to a controllable level during the actual performance. After performance, surprisingly, anxiety level is higher than at any time either prior to or during the performance. A good example of higher post-performance anxiety level would be NASCAR drivers. Many times they have had accidents or didn't perform well in a race and they're post-performance anxiety level is incredible high, and reporters try to ask them questions before they even get out of the car. This has caused some real problems, because they don't give the drivers time to back off emotionally. When I worked with a NASCAR driver a few years ago, the one thing we did was to keep reporters away until at least ten minutes following the race. This gave the driver a chance to get back under control emotionally. This happens in a lot of other environments also. It happens in the business environment, it happens in families where conversations become emotional and either the parents or children get over the edge emotionally and the end result is that conversation serves no purpose. I often suggest that when people sit down to talk, knowing how important emotional level is, that they make an objective list of things to be discussed. When the conversation becomes emotional, they can look at the list and go back to something objective. This helps them stay as productive as possible.

There are many things involved with controlling your emotions. There are things that will be discussed later in this chapter such as having a fear of success and a fear of failure, both of which are emotional issues and have nothing to do with talent. There are situations where people have lost their physical abilities to do their routine daily tasks and therefore they become very emotional, and over a period of time they almost lose their emotions, which is very devastating. It makes emotion a fun topic to talk about, but we really need to make sure that we understand how to control our emotions and understand how to raise and lower our emotions when necessary. We talked about motivation. Motivation is simply a process of raising and lowering your emotional level to a point that is productive, but not to the point where it causes a person to try to over-perform. In other words, don't try too hard to perform. One of the most common problems that people have when you talk about their emotions is that they think too much. They over-analyze. If there's any question about performance, they make it more complicated than it should be. When you do these things, you're basically throwing away energy that can be used in a more productive way. If you're emotionally over the edge, you are much more likely to become physically and mentally fatigued, causing a detriment to your physical performance.

Now, the two most interesting areas that deal with emotion that also relate to getting the mud out of the water are fear of success and fear of failure. There are indications that you may have a fear of success if you put yourself in certain situations that almost dictate that you won't succeed. In other words, do you avoid the really tough visible assignments? Are you really not challenged in your job, yet you avoid promotion? Have you seen athletes who are not what we call pressure-players? We say that some athletes are practice players and some are gamers. Do you find that the higher-up people advance in a company the more they are criticized? Do you consistently root for under-dogs in sports? Are you just afraid to succeed? I've worked with athletes who had tremendous physical talent who never made it simply because they were afraid to succeed. Many tennis players and golfers with incredible talent are happy to play the number 2 or number 3 position on a team because it's an easy way to avoid the accountability that comes with being number

1. How many people do you know in middle management positions who are afraid to risk being better? They are afraid to accept the consequences of their actions required at the executive level. How many housewives are subconsciously reluctant to manage their time in order to be more productive personally? We can take a valuable lesson from youngsters. They move ahead with reckless abandon. They like to succeed until we tell them how lonely it is that the top. We almost cause some kids to have a fear of success. The bottom line is that if we don't succeed, it's usually because we don't want to succeed.

Why would anyone be afraid to succeed? It seems silly, but many people are content to survive. To be contributors, but certainly not leaders. Many athletes never reach the top because of the visibility, or the responsibility or the higher expectations and increased accountability. Business people suffer from the same dilemma as athletes. If you are one of those people who play well, but don't win, then I have a plan for you.

1. Evaluate your talent. If you decide you want to win, do you have the talent to win?

2. Decide if you're willing to pay the price of success, to be evaluated daily, to make the tough decisions and to be accountable.

3. Ask yourself if there's a path open for you to succeed. If not, then you need to explore the steps necessary for creating a path for your advancement, and that may mean a different environment. We've talked before about the importance of the environment in performance. Many

times people can't get the mud out of the water and clear their minds because there are too many extraneous factors floating in the environment and they can't rid themselves of these issues. Many times a simple change of environment will get the mud out of the water for you.

4. Ask yourself when you will know if you've succeeded. A lot of people talk about recovery and succeeding but they don't know what they are recovering to, or even when they have succeeded. It's important that you have specific plans and goals in place so you know when you got there. If you have the talent and you're willing to be visible and there is a plan, then you need to spend time writing what I call "success actions", leading you to succeed. Measureable, specific, attainable actions. Give yourself a realistic yet demanding time table.

5. Determine who can help you and discuss your plan with these people. Go back to the chapter on building a team and review that information constantly. There are many instances where you might have a fear of success because of certain deficiencies. In that situation you should put team members in place who can help you over those deficiencies. Take time to taste the small successes on the way to the big one. Oh yeah, don't forget reward yourself when you reach a benchmark!

6. Be persistent. Be totally committed. Everyone in every environment can and should settle for nothing short of success.

Fear of success is a real issue, but it's discussed very little, because common sense would say, "Why would you not want to succeed?" The fact is that a lot of people are simply afraid to be successful because they don't want to be perceived as a leader. At the other end of the spectrum, we have fear of failure. I think everyone has had a fear of failing at some time in some task whether it's complex or simple. That's just a part of human nature and a part of life. Fear of failure can actually be an incentive to performance. A motivator to performance until it reaches a certain point. Now, we need to realize that fear of failure runs along a scale like emotions, from one to ten. Fear of failure can motivate you but you can reach a point where fear of failure gets so significant that you withdraw from a task. It's easy to spot. What people typically do with a fear of failure is accept challenges that nobody could perform and so failure is okay and you're not accountable, or they accept only the easiest tasks which only require you to breathe to be successful. How do you know if you have a fear of failure? Normally it's because, the types of tasks that people select to do are just enough to surviveregardless of talent. Maybe you don't want to put yourself on the line so that the probability of failure is much higher than you can deal with. Winners have a fear of failure, there's no question. The consistent winners are those who have learned to recover from failure and recover quickly. They don't let the fear of failure dictate their performance. My major challenge is dealing with athletes who have been successful all their lives with no failure and suddenly they've begun to lose. This happens not only in sports, but in business and family environments. It happens with people who have chronic illnesses as in my case. It happens with me sometimes with MS. I want to do things many times because I have a fear of failure and I've never been used to failing. I've been used to succeeding my whole life. So I've had to train myself to accept the failure in order to become better. Golf is a good example. When I was diagnosed with MS I had to quit playing golf because my balance was so bad. Now, I've begun to play again and probably play better than ever because I'm not concerned with another issue other than making contact with the ball. It's made me swing slower and appreciate the game more. But it would have been easy for me, because of the fear of failure, to sell my clubs and never play again. If you feel that you have a significant fear of failure issue, then plan to take steps immediately. In this, time is not your friend. It doesn't get better over time.

1. Examine your goals and matching task to achieve success. Review the chapter dealing with goals so that you know they are specific and they are difficult, but most of all, they are attainable. Make sure that you set attainable goals. Psychologically, it's better to attain them and raise them than to not be able to achieve them and have to lower then.

2. Divide tasks into subtasks. In other words, appreciate the steps along the way to execution. Appreciate the process and what it takes to put all the parts together to achieve a task. Know that you will be successful in some parts and unsuccessful in others. But give yourself credit for being successful in some of the tasks.

3. Put a specific time table on each subtask. Again, time is not your friend. You need to press the issue time-wise.

4. Have at least one thing to accomplish every day.

5. Reward yourself when you accomplish the subtask. Don't wait until the process is over. Reward yourself along the way because this gives you incentive to pursue the task.

6. As accomplishments become more consistent, then you can add some complexity to the task.

Just remember, and it's been mentioned a couple of times, if you don't make mistakes, you're probably not being productive and if you're not being productive, then you are just surviving at best. If you want to succeed, if you want to get better and do things that give you a better self-image and self-concept, then you owe it to yourself to supplement your talent with positive emotion. We go back and we review chapters dealing with expectations. If your expectations are very low, then maybe you have a fear of failure. If you expectations are incredible high, maybe you have a fear of success. So you need to put yourself in a position where you realize every single day that whatever you did that day was worth getting up in the morning and in doing so you realize that every day is a blessing. Every day you have an opportunity to do something you haven't done the day before. You CANNOT do that unless you use your emotions in a positive way.

CHAPTER 9

Be Motivated,
But be Careful

Regardless of the type of motivation that's used, timing is probably the most important aspect of motivation. Motivation at an inappropriate time is no more valuable than the entire absence of motivation. In fact, it may be more harmful to performance than no motivation at all. Poorly timed efforts at motivation have an artificial air about them. To be effective, motivation must occur when the person being motivated will most benefit from a feeling of recognition, belonging, or success. As I have noted in earlier chapters, many times the activity itself will motivate a person. In sports, golf is a good example. Some people participate in golf, not to compete, but because golf itself presents a challenge; the reason being every shot is different. One good shot will motivate players to continue to play. You often hear at golf courses that if you hit one great shot in a round of golf, which may consist of 90 to 100 shots, that one good shot will bring you back to play again. You need to be able to transfer that attitude to your daily environment so that if you do several things that don't work or don't go well, but we do one thing well, that one thing will be enough of an incentive to get me motivated for the next day. So we need to recognize those little things as they come to us. There are several different ways to motivate.

Need to explore is the complexity of what you are trying to do and the motivation necessary to do that. For example, in a highly complex skill, it's probably better to be moderately motivated because of all the information that you have to process. So you don't want to be, in other words, emotionial over the edge if you're performing something that's really complex. Now, in relatively simply skills, daily skills like walking and eating, those kinds of skills, we can be at a higher level of motivation because the skill complexity is much less and there's much less information to process. So the type of motivation is important in regard to what the motivation is meant to do, whether it's intrinsic or extrinsic. There are probably times when we use both types of motivation, but for long-term results, I don't think there's any question that intrinsic motivation is much more valuable for long-term impact. The timing is obviously important. It's almost like with children when we talk about critical learning periods. There are critical times, which we call teachable moments with children, when they reach a certain level emotionally, socially and physically, where the package comes together and it's an appropriate time for them to learn certain kinds of skills.

Those are critical learning periods. I think in adults many times there are still critical periods where motivation is either going to be appropriate or inappropriate based on where the person is psychologically at that time. We never want motivation to come across as being insincere or superficial. It should always be used at a time when it's accepted as being honest and when it's accepted as being an effort to help a person to improve and to accomplish things that they haven't done recently. This is especially true with people with chronic illness. It's very important that if you are going to be motivated to do anything, that you have to get recognized as was mentioned in the first chapter of this book, recognize "the mud in the water." In other words, understand the things that are on your mind and don't get caught up in being motivated to remove all that clutter at one time. We have to prioritize the mud in the water and then we have an incentive to work with each item, either to work with it, store it away or to learn to live with it. You can't look at the whole package at one time. You have to take each factor that's perceived as "mud in your water" and deal with them individually and set up an action so that you're motivated to accomplish something specific with each factor.

Now to put all this in perspective in real life and to put it in a nutshell, motivation really stirs your system. Motivation is a psychological phenomenon that has physio-logical impacts on your system. In other words, you get emotional, you get anxious and once your emotions reach a certain level then you are motivated to accomplish some task. It's interesting that motivation is one of the most often talked about concepts as was previously mentioned, but probably the most misunderstood. Over my 40 years in working with athletes, the first question I get in meetings is how do you motivate athletes? My response has always been that in my 40 years in working with athletes or working with corporate people, I have never attempted to motivate.

Motivation is really just a way of arousing your system. We've talked about the mechanics of motivation, the types of motivation, but in real life, motivation is trying to accomplish something every single day. In other words, if you get up in the morning and you've written down something for the day and you have goals, then those goals provide you with incentive to accomplish something during that day. People are either motivated to accomplish something, or they are motivated to not fail. I have very little patience with people who are motivated to not fail. I think that those people are pretty scary to be around and they live their lives in a very superficial way. You need to be motivated to accomplish something every single day. In other words, there are no guarantees in life, but if you're motivated to get up and to try to walk or to get some mud out of the water or whatever it might be, then at least the probability is on your side that you're going to accomplish that. Those things don't really happen by mistake and so you have to have directed energy and directed emotion in order to accomplish things. One of the problems I have with people who go into support meetings, those people with chronic illness, is that many times support meetings are filled with other patients who feel so bad and want everybody else to know how bad their feel. That being the case, people who go into those meetings feeling pretty good, leave the meeting feeling pretty bad because nothing positive happened during the meeting. My suggestion to folks who have support meetings in whatever area of life it may be is that if you don't leave a meeting with something in hand that will at least give you a chance to do more tomorrow or to feel better tomorrow or to accomplish something that you didn't do today, then you're in the wrong meeting. People who are motivated to accomplish something in life are risk takers. They are willing to fail, but they're also able to recover quickly. People who are motivated to not fail accomplish very little in their lives. And so it's very important that you understand the difference in extrinsic and intrinsic motivation, the difference in needs and drives and the other mechanics of motivation so that you can develop a plan to accomplish, a plan to move ahead in your life. As an MS patient, there are times when I might be motivated tomorrow to walk a mile. Well, there are no guarantees, but at least that's my incentive is to try to walk a mile. If I don't, at least I've given the effort and I can feel good about the effort and I can go further the next day than I did today. But without motivation, with a sense of fulfillment or belong, or self-esteem, then I'm not going to be motivated to accomplish very much. So everybody who reads this chapter needs to understand that motivation is basic to accomplish goals and live life in a very fulfilling way. Without motivation, without incentive, without writing things down, without having specific goals, there's very little probability that you're ever going to accomplish what you're capable of doing because your motivation is going to be helter-skelter and it's going to be off track. You need to be directed so that you're energy is used in a very productive and positive manner.

INTRINSIC MOTIVATORS

1. _____

2. _____

3. _____

4. _____

5. _____

6. _____

7. _____

8. _____

9. _____

10. _____

EXTRINSIC MOTIVATORS

1. _____

2. _____

3. _____

4. _____

5. _____

6. _____

7. _____

8. _____

9. _____

10. _____

Get a Good Coach

A good coach is a nice asset to have when you're struggling to get the mud out of the water. You need somebody with an objective perspective on where you are and where you want to go. They're not easy to find. It's a real advantage to find a good coach and to keep that coach. Given equal talent in sports, for example, mental development through directional coaching separates the elite performers from the good performers. There are tremendous benefits to having good directional coaching. More productivity is probably an obvious benefit. Better balance, which is one of those intangible benefits that is hard to realize sometimes, but better balance both personally and professionally are tremendous assets for you to pursue. Better performance, better team performance and in the case of those folks who have coaches as individuals, then it's obviously better performance on your part. There are pre-requisites if you are to select a coach. There are certainly pre-requisites that a coach must have in regard to those people that he or she is coaching. One is recognition of assets and liabilities of those being coached and as we mentioned early in the book in Chapter 2, you have to recognize your assets and liabilities which is not an easy task when you're struggling with "mud in the water," clutter in your mind. But you need to list those and share those with a coach. The coach needs to have an understanding of who's on the team, not just the players, but the people surrounding the players. Coaches understand also that just being better than others doesn't guarantee winning. If you're pursuing the leadership from a coach as a team, coaches need to help you understand that just being better than your competitors doesn't make you a winner, it just makes you better than another group of people and that winners are those who pursue their goals and work their plan and let the competitor watch them. And coaches need to understand the talent on the team. Basically what we have discussed in this text deals with emotional well-being and emotional control of people, but regardless of how good you feel and how much control you have over your emotions and how easily you're able to get the mud out of the water, talent is certainly pre-requisite to winning. Also coaches need to be able to work with people, certainly on-call and on a one-to-one basis. In the corporate environment, you see coaches visit executives and visit the work force on occasion, but a true coach needs to be on call, needs to be available when crisis comes, needs to be available when a person's struggling to get the mud out of the water. It does very little good to have issues on Monday and then talk with your coach on Friday. If you have issues on Monday, then you certainly need to talk with your coach on Monday. I think the job of a coach many times is misunderstood and in the corporate environment, there's a tendency to use coaching and training interchangeably which is certainly a misconception. Training deals with basic learning. Coaching deals with tweaking your system, creating a good environment and several other things that will be discussed later. A job as a coach carries with it certain responsibilities; one of those is to create an environment in which the players are free to play and make the coach look good. As we discussed in a previous chapter, the worst thing to have is over-coaching because then you develop coach-conscious players. So a coach needs to do everything possible to avoid developing coach-conscious players. Coaches must be committed to coaching and developing the team including, but not limited to, the following areas. Coaches need to deal with personality, with chemistry, with letting leaders on the team lead the team, with helping players develop pride in themselves and the team, with helping players develop a burning desire to win. A lot of people have never won so it's very difficult to develop a burning desire to win if you don't know what it feels like to win. So coaches need to spoon-feed in many cases so people understanding how good it tastes to accomplish something. Coaches need to teach players how to recover quickly from adversity which has been discussed in the text. Coaches need to teach players how to use what has been mentioned as a "timed mental lapse". In other words, teach players how to give themselves a mental break. It's ridiculous to think that you can go into a zone for a long period of time because your system won't let you do that. Your system will take a break whether you like it or not. So you need to learn to take a break when you want a break as opposed to taking a mental break when your system decides it needs a break. Coaches need to teach the difference between motivation and achievement motivation which I think is a critical area for coaching. A lot of coaches deliver motivational speeches and rant and rave and carry on to get teams excited, but that has a very limited impact over the course of a contest. Initially, it raises your emotions and your anxiety level, but once the competition starts, it doesn't have that much of a positive impact. You have to be achievement motivated; in other words, motivated by the prospects of achieving something specific. A good coach uses both intrinsic an extrinsic motivation, both of which have been discussed extensively in this text. A coach may be most important, especially in big events, needs to teach a team to thrive on stress. You see very good teams with talented players fold under stress and so many times teams with average talent will be successful because emotionally they're able to look forward to and to use stress as an incentive to performance. A coach needs to help you break your goals down and work backward to today. We mentioned in a chapter previous to this how important it is to set goals and then to back those goals up so that you are able to stay on tract every day and a good coach can help you to do that. A good coach needs to allow players to reward themselves and encourage players to reward themselves without regard to the size or the significance of the win. In other words, if you win a game, obviously that's a big achievement. If you have some type of disability and you do something today that you were not able to do yesterday that's just as big an achievement and so you need to reward yourself for achievements. A coach can help you and encourage you to do that. As has been mentioned, rewarding yourself gives you recognition for what you accomplish today and also leads you into tomorrow with positive expectations. I think a major asset of a good coach is basic communication. Coaches need to communicate person-to-person, eye to-eye, as opposed to texting. I don't put much stock in quick motivational messages that are delivered through an e-mail or a text. There's nothing more effective than having person-to-person, open, honest communication. Most coaches who are good coaches are also willing to be coached. There are times when you select a coach to help you where you're going to be in a position to help them become better coaches. So I've always said that a good coach is a person who's also willing to be coached. I think a good coach also understands that no one over-achieves, we just get closer to our capabilities. It bothers me every time I hear someone described as an over-achiever. I think if someone told me I had over-achieved, I would be bothered because my perception would then be that they didn't think I was very good when we started. I'd rather us talk about people getting closer to their potential, closer to their capabilities, not as over achievers. Lastly, I think coaches help players match their goals to their assets. You're probably able to do that at this point if you've followed the text. But it's still helps to have a coach review and help you match your goals to your assets. Anytime you're setting goals and you get a little emotional, then your goals might be unfair in regard to matching your assets. Be proud of your assets and be proud of the goals that those assets allow you to accomplish. If you were to interview very successful coaches, I think one of the first things they would say is that their job is to help players to "get the mud out of the water." In other words, to help the players clear their minds so that they can focus, concentrate, and recover quickly from adversity. Now this is certainly an extensive list of the things that coaches should be able to do, but it's certainly not an inclusive list. There are other things that are unique to different environments for coaches to be able to do but it seems that in many cases, as in other disciplines, many coaches try too hard. We've talked about over-coaching and there's nothing worse than trying too hard at any thing you do. If you want to get up and walk, if you have trouble walking with balance, if you want to walk, you really have to have a mindset that you are going to let yourself walk. As an MS patient, many days I don't feel that I'm very mobile, but I don't try to make myself walk a long distance. I get up with the intent of walking and from that point I let myself walk. I don't force the issue. If you try too hard at almost anything you are going to be less successful. A good coach is a person who can be around you and help you understand that. A good coach can really watch you and be able to recognize if you're trying too hard to perform. I've seen pitchers who would throw 95 miles an hour in the bull pen and go into the game trying to throw 96 and throw only 88. They really become confused. I had one pitcher come to me after the first inning of a game and said there must be something wrong with the pitching mound because I was throwing 95 before and now I'm throwing 88. My comment to him was, "Hey, you're trying too hard. You're locking up your system. You're not letting yourself go through a full easy range of motion."

And so it's very common for coaches to try too hard, especially coaches who are dealing with people who may have disabilities and require good supportive coaching. Many coaches feel that they need to prove their worth as opposed to many times just being there and being able to answer questions and talk about issues. That's as much a part of coaching as the instructional side. In working with corporations and sports teams for the last 39 years, there are certain characteristics that seem to recur with successful coaches, and again, it's not inclusive, it includes some of those things we've talked about, but some of those coaches have many characteristics that I think are worth mentioning here.

Coaches are excellent teachers. They are knowledgeable about players, about business, about you personally, and more importantly they create an environment which encourages learning. If a coach understands the business that you are involved in, they they will have ideas that are beneficial in that business. In sports, many of your better coaches were not your great athletes, because the great athletes, everything came so easy for them, they don't understand how difficult it is to play the game. Many of your great coaches were those who never made it to the highest level of their sport, but they were students of the game. It's so important that a coach be a student of the game. If you have a disability, and my point of reference is obviously MS because I'm a patient, if I'm going to have a coach work for me, then I need that coach to understand that even though I may look fine at many times I don't feel fine. The coach needs to understand all the characteristics of MS so they are not only compassionate about what may be going on with me on a particular day, but they are encouraging and they have some ideas, or they may have a possible solution. For example, if I'm having cognitive issues, the coach needs to be a person who will tell me sit down every day for an hour on the computer and play games to keep your wheels turning. I found that in my case playing FreeCell and Solitaire and other games on the computer really gives me an indication of how sharp I am mentally on that day. I think it's critical that coaches have a genuine humanistic approach to whomever they are coaching. I think coaches need to respect what the players bring to the environment. Also, they need to realize that things outside the work place influence production. They need to realize the importance of balance. It's very important that coaches realize what assets you have in the environment and maybe some assets that you've lost. They can help you to regain some of those assets, or be able to come up with ideas and alternatives to those assets which might make you just as productive as you were before. When you're looking to select your coach, whether it's personally or for your team, it's very important that you select someone who has these previously mentioned characteristics, but also someone who is liberal with positive reinforcement as opposed to having reinforcement be the exception. There are coaches who spend so much time using what they like to call "negative reinforcement" or "negative motivation" that they end up working so hard at trying to rebuild players after they've worn them out mentally that they almost get coaching-brain-drain. There's no excuse for ever getting brain-drain in coaching. Coaching should be fun, it should be an honor. You should realize that people hire you as a coach or select you because you have something they need, something that you can use to reinforce them.

You know, we've talked about the nitty-gritty characteristics that coaches have and only a couple of the intangible qualities, but I think if I were selecting a coach today, I would suggest that they go to two places before they coach me. One would be to a playground and watch kids play. I've never seen, I don't think, a better environment for learning about cooperation, competition, leadership and all those other things that go into providing a winning environment than what kids show you on a playground. They work together, they put creativity into practical use, a quality that we seem to lose as we get older. When I ask groups how many people are as creative as they were when they were kids, no one raises their hand. In reality everyone is as creative as they were when they were kids. It's just that when we become adults, we become more reserved are no willing to do risk-taking kinds of things or things that might be perceived as out of the ordinary. You can learn creativity watching kids. They choose leaders, they make rules, and they play the game and have fun. They have arguments, they fight, get over it and go eat a hot dog and drink a soft drink. Life goes on. They don't carry the grudges we carry. The playground is a wonderful place to learn about how people interact with each other. The other place I would suggest that my coach visit would be home for senior citizens. I think it's the most valuable asset we have in this country and the most neglected. You hear many corporate people behind closed doors talk about older people being dead wood in a corporation. My response to that is that wood dies due to a lack of nutrition. We don't use those people and the knowledge they have. Older people in a senior home is not going to tell you about computers and sales and marketing, but they can tell you how to live to be an older person. I read an article the other day and a 106 year-old woman in Canada was the life of her birthday party. She talked about her diet which she credits for helping her live that long. Her diet consists of pizza, French fries and sweets. You certainly wouldn't recommend it, but who's to say it didn't work for her? I've talked to old people who have told me they take a drink and smoke a cigar every day. Well, you know, that has worked for them. They tell you how to get along with people and how to get along in this world. Those are assets that we are gradually losing in the corporate environment as well as the educational environment and in almost every other social environment we have because technology has basically taken over. We text, we e-mail, we fax. We don't really talk with one another. To me, it's impossible to coach if you don't talk with people. I want a coach who is familiar with the span of life, a coach who understands children and what older people bring to the party. I want a coach who will remind me of the intangible things that I may have lost track of because of things that have gone on in the work place or because I have a devastating disease. I may have lost track of some important intangible things that I had before I got the disease. So I need a coach who will put me back in touch with real life issues that will help me achieve what I need to do and where I need to go in life.

After I decide what I need in a coach, then it's necessary to sit down and look at the people you know. People who are friends, acquaintances or associates in the workplace. You need to select someone whom you can communicate with at any time, day or night, seven days a week if need be. And the person you select must be willing to be there for you. Coaches are something that we need to do a better job of selecting for disabled folks. We call them caretakers. Caretakers are coaches and we need to educate caretakers so that they are able to take on a coaching personality and understand what they are doing and why they are doing it. If you've gotten to this point in the book, the you understand how important assets and liabilities and goals are, and thriving on stress and expecting to win, and all the other things we've talked about that are going to make your life better, and certainly they will enable you to get the mud out of the water. I think the icing on the cake is to find a good coach, your very own coach who is committed to helping you go where you want to go in life.

I've been a mental coach for almost 40 years and I can honestly say that I've learned something every year, and maybe even every day, over those 40 years about working with individuals and helping them to realize their potential. I can also say that I've done it using the techniques I've discussed in this text. I start Chapter 1 and I go straight through the end of the book with every person and athlete I work with. We work at it and I'm totally committed to helping ever single client to become not only more self-sufficient, but to become more appreciative of the talent they have and find the talent they've forgotten they have. It's a rewarding feeling to see people accomplish something they did not think they could. Once they get the mud out of the water and compartmentalize and use the other techniques in their lives, it's rewarding to see what they are able to accomplish.

COACH CHARACTERISTICS

(TO MEET YOUR NEEDS)

1. _____

2. _____

3. _____

4. _____

5. _____

6. _____

7. _____

8. _____

9. _____

10. _____

CHAPTER 11

Winning vs Surviving: Getting the Mud Out of the Water

Winners are made, not born. A very old cliché which applies here is simply "you can win if you're willing to pay the price." That is true in most cases. When we talk about winners versus survivors, it's very easy until we begin to discuss those things which separate the winners from the survivors. Very often, the winners do little things to push them over the top. Things which we may not see until a game is over, the day is over, or until the task is over. In business, the true winners not only talk the game, but execute the winning ways. Winning can be contagious if it's given a chance. Basically, winning deals with the interaction with several areas often dealt with in the work place. Winning can be attached to very simply things such as being able to walk across the room, even making a bed if you have a chronic illness. Winning can be realized if you know at the end of the day you did everything you could possibly do at a task regardless of the outcome. In your life, the quality of the interaction as well as the fine-tuning of the environment, are crucial to winning consistently. Every player has a role to play on your team, and many times more than one role to play in order for the team to win. Again, as was discussed early in this book, selecting the appropriate players to help you win is critical. A quick review of winning habits every time the feeling begins to wane will help you sustain a higher level of performance. Don't misunderstand this list. These factors apply in every part of your life. These are not sport factors that deal with winning, they are life factors.

1. Winners expect to win every day. In other words, winners buck the system by expecting to be successful. We've talked before about the fact that children are told approximately 200,000 by the time they are 18 years old what not to do. Therefore, they come out into the world assuming that if they avoid failure, that winning will be a natural outcome which, as we know, is not true. Your plan should be based on what you expect to gain instead of what you expect to avoid. Many times this posture, once it becomes habit, results in a major attitudinal upheaval and most importantly this attitude of expecting to achieve something every day at least puts the probability of success on your side at whatever you may be trying to accomplish.

2. Winners have a positive mental attitude. I've always told groups don't feel good for no reason because it doesn't last for very long. Have a positive mental attitude

because you are good at something. In other words, you need a positive mental attitude in your life in order to have positive expectations, but at the same time, you need reinforcement constantly for that positive attitude, which means you may have to back up in your task on occasion and accomplish simpler tasks in order to regain that positive attitude. Don't get bogged down by not being able to perform something that's very complex.

3. Winners play every day at as high an emotional level as they can control. In the chapter which dealt with stretching your emotions every day, it should be obvious how important your emotional state is to winning every day. It's a part of winning. We should be proud of our emotions and willing to share our emotions with other people. We become emotionally fatigued when we constantly relax and recover, so it's to your advantage to maintain a high level of emotion every day in whatever you are trying to accomplish. If you go over the edge emotionally, have something in your mental bag, which was discussed before, to get you back to the edge. If you are able to sustain a higher level of emotion, you don't suffer from the fatigue of having to recover back to the edge so many times on a given day.

4. Winners thrive on stress. Again, this was talked about in a previous chapter dealing with stress and anxiety. Stress can be a wonderful thing if you can control the stressors. Just to review, 80% of stress is probably neither good nor bad when it comes to your system. We

make stress negative in our reactions to it. The key is to focus your energy which has traditionally been spent on combating stress—you need to focus that energy on using stress as an incentive to become better. Winners are what you call the true tension seekers. In my case, being an MS patient I have a lot of stress in my life. So every day, I try to use those stressors to enable me to accomplish things, that when the day started, I may not have thought I could do. Even though I'm not able to accomplish everything, at least I'm able to accomplish some things because of the way that I perceive stress as being an asset as opposed to a liability.

5. Winners have specific goals. We've talked many times about the importance of setting goals and we've talked about the fact that doing the best you can is an easy way out, but certainly not a beneficial way to approach every day. Winners know every day exactly what they want to achieve within a specific time frame. Again, goals needs to be specific, difficult and attainable, so at the end of the day when you accomplish something, a goal that you had set out to accomplish, then you are able to reward yourself. Rewards give you credibility for all the things you did in a given day, but also take you to the next day with positive expectations.

6. Winners realize the importance of teamwork. There was a whole chapter devoted to selecting your team. The folks who can not only supplement your assets, but also the folks who can replace your liabilities. It's so impor-

tant that every player know their role on the team and that they can execute that role. They won't know that unless you have good, open, honest communications with all the players on your team.

7. Winners communicate with team members, not to team members. There is an old cliché worth repeating here that was mentioned earlier: what you are speaks so loud, people can't hear what you say. Very simply that means that your body language communicates to your team members. Your gestures communicate and, obviously, your verbiage communicates to team members. All of these things must be used in a very positive and constructive way so that every communication is truly a conversation and not a one-sided instructional time.

8. In winning environments, management is tolerant of mistakes made while trying to succeed. If you don't make mistakes, then you are probably not accomplishing much. A certain amount of trial and error learning is significantly beneficial in the retention of whatever skill it might be that you are trying to accomplish. There is nothing more harmful to development then creating an error-free environment where people are not permitted to have adversity and therefore never learn how to recover from adversity. A very simple rule to follow is if you are going to make a mistake, make it trying to move forward; don't make it backing over things. At least your energy is spent in trying to get better.

9. Coaches must provide players with a winning environment. In other words, you need to be in an environment that motivates you as opposed to having people around you all the time who are trying to motivate you. That's wasted energy with only short-term results. Motivating the environment for example, changing the colors of rooms, furniture, changing the lighting, changing pictures; all these things have an impact on motivation. There have been studies in industries for 70, 80 years that indicate that a change in environment which indicates that someone cares about those folks in the environment causes an improvement in productivity. This is true not only in the business environment. It's true in the sports environment and in the home environment. For those people who have disabilities, if the team members in support of that person can change things around, paint the walls, help you make your environment better and more comfortable and "homier" feeling to you, then you are going to feel better and you're going to be much more productive in the environment.

10. Winners hold their focus and are able to change their focus quickly. We talked about developing a plan before and how important it is to have a plan, but also we talked about the fact that a plan has to be flexible. There almost has to be in many environments, because no environment is perfect. There has to be a plan B. There has to be an alternative. There has to be, in many cases, different ways to accomplish the same goal. The focus of a good plan is directed on the present and the future.

It's not directed on avoiding the past. Having a focus within your plan at least keeps you on track emotionally, so that you don't veer off track and spend a lot of energy recovering back to the lack of the plan.

11. When focus is lost, winners are able to recover quickly. Now, we just talked about the importance of having a focus, the importance of having a plan, but many times there are things that happen during a performance or during a task that you're undertaking at home that don't always go according to pain. Many times, heat is a detriment to performance for those who have disabilities. Many times just the stress of pursuing a task will cause a plan to be off track. Many times there are distractions. Extraneous things in the environment that are obviously unexpected may interrupt the plan. Those things are a part of real life and will happen. The important thing to remember here is the plan. The basic process to get back to the plan as soon as possible. In other words, to recovery. We've talked many times about the fact that recovery is not the issue, because everyone can recover. The issue is speed of recovery. So you need to develop in your mental bag, things that will enable you to recover back to the plan much more quickly.

12. Winners reward themselves. I just mentioned previously that when you achieve goals or when you at least move in the direction of a positive outcome, you should reward yourself. Reward yourself for effort, if you will, as well as rewarding yourself for accomplishment.

Small rewards for achievement of steps toward longer term goals are critical. It's not the reward itself. Self reward is a legitimate vehicle for sustaining motivation, but it's not the reward, it's the concept. A reward was given to a national women's fast pitch softball team in the last year, there were two rewards given after each game. The players selected an award winner and the coach selected a winner. The award was a penny. It was incredible how the players reacted to that penny. So it was the concept. Over the years, there have been many coaches, university coaches, especially in swimming, who have used daily rewards. Many years ago at the top university for developing swimmers in the United States; the reward after swimming a good practice lap was an M&M. The M&M meant the world to the swimmers! So it's the concept. The reward is the concept. It's not an extrinsic reward that is actually material gain. It's more recognition for what you've done.

13. Winning environments are not havens for survivors. With an increased emphasis, especially in the corporate environment on getting more from fewer people, traditional survivors must begin to develop a taste for winning. In other words, as a company gets better and moves to a higher level, those folks who were survivors previously are going to be left behind. Those folks who are complacent are not going to be able to stay in that work environment. Many times, there are teams in which a player who may be a great player may have to be replaced because they don't fit the chemistry of the

team. In that particular environment, they've abandoned winning and become survivors. It doesn't make them bad people, they just need to be back in an environment where they are motivated to win and maybe have more emphasis on their personal performance. It's very important that you constantly evaluate your team, your professional team, and your personal team in order to keep the team strong. There may need to be changes periodically to keep the team strong because as you're team gets weaker, so do you. In keeping with the philosophy put forth in this book, we all need to "get the mud out of the water" and have people around us who can help us get the mud out of the water, clear our minds, move ahead and accomplish something every day. You have to have a strong team around you every day in order to do that.

14. Coaches win because players want them to win. On the surface that may not make much sense, but it's true. The good coaches are those who put the players in a position to make them look good and in a position in which they can play well. You must have as a team a burning desire to help each other win. A coach many times sets the tone for that attitude. If you have a coach who's working with you, it's very important that your coach knows from you what motivates you, what your expectations are, what your environmental needs are, what your training needs are so that you can perform better. Everybody I think can use coaching if it's productive coaching. To me, over-coaching is worse than

no coaching at all. The worse thing that can happen is that you become a "coach-conscious" player. Coach-conscious players are those players who are always conscious that they are being watched. If they make a mistake, they look at the coach. If they don't perform well over time, they look at the coach. If something's wrong on the team, they look at the coach. Therefore, their productivity is hindered because half of their energy is being spent as a coach-conscious player. If you have a disability, your challenges are strong enough so that you don't need the added burden of having a coach around you that makes you coach-conscious. So coaches are important if they're good.

15. Winners have balance. This is a topic that is not discussed as much as it should be in seminars and in company environments. Consistent winners recognize the importance of fulfillment, both personally and professionally. Winners evaluate balance in terms of quality of time spent, not quantity of time spent. There are so many, in fact too many to list here, corporate executives that I've worked with over the years who have no balance in their lives. If you look from the outside looking in at their accomplishments, you're first thought is that they are very successful and they are winners. But when you really evaluate them, you find that their personal lives are in shambles and, to me, they're losers. Unless you win both personally and professionally in your life, then you cannot claim to be a winner. If material gain is the most important thing in your life and how much

money that you're going to make, then you're a very superficial person. If you have balance in your life, you realize that for everything you do professionally is because of something that you want to support personally. There's no substitute for family. No friendships will be as strong for you as family. So those of you who work 13, 14, or 15 hours a day, you're stealing time from the very side of life that causes you to do what you do. Under this circumstance, you're likely to wake up one day and hate your job because it's stolen from you the things that were important to you in your personal life. So balance is a real key that many times is disregarded in the corporate environment.

16. Winners never apologize for being good. When I talk with MS patient groups, I tell them, never apologize for being good. If you can walk three miles, be proud to talk about walking three miles. If you can ride a mountain bike race, be proud to talk about it and don't think that you should feel bad about being able to accomplish things. I think many times we are too humble, and in the process of being humble, we lose some of our self-confidence and our self-esteem because we feel like many times we do not deserve what we're getting out of life. Most of the time, you'll find that people who are successful and people who can accomplish certain things in life are able succeed because they have a history of hard work, a history of training and a history of commitment. So never ever, ever apologize for being good at what you do.

17. Winners are totally committed to winning. In other words, have a burning desire to win. Winners use all their assets in an effort to accomplish something every single day. Winners never let their liabilities roll over onto their assets. Winners are those who build their lives around the things they can accomplish and then eventually not only accomplish more, but eliminate some of their liabilities. This is especially true for those with disabilities and chronic illnesses. If we thought more about the things we can accomplish and less about the things that drive us nuts, then we would be able to do more, and we would feel better about who we are. We have to have pride in who we are and what we bring to the party every day.

In summary, I would say that this chapter encompasses the concept of the whole book. I would also say that if you are totally committed to doing things you haven't been able to do in the past, if you are totally committed to getting the "mud out of the water" in your life and moving ahead, you are going to realize that the pride you have is unequaled in your life previously. You are going to feel better about who you are and better about what you do. It's going to be a fun ride from this day forward!

CHAPTER 12

Wrapping it Up

Well, that's the plan! Now it's time to put the finishing touches on what I hope has been an informative and worthwhile project for you. It certainly has benefitted me to go through this process and putting on paper what I've been practicing with my adversities and all the mud I've had in the water. It's been a tremendous help to me. There are a few points that I want to finish with.

One of them is something that you don't learn in seminars and you certainly can't learn by making lists and setting things on paper. It deals with pride. Everybody has pride, but for some reason, we are not willing to show it. I've never understood that and I think we need to make a conscious effort. Once you get the mud out of the water and begin to move forward with your lives, I think it's very important that you begin to show pride in who you are and pride in what you bring to the party every day. You need to decide what pushes your button. It may be in the short term that money and material gain is important, but really matters is what's best for you in the long term. That is why I spent so much time in one chapter talking about intrinsic motivation. You need to understand why you do what you do. I think you'll find if you are honest with yourself, it's not for material gain. In sports, pride is a tremendous motivator. Players play hurt because of pride. Pride causes players to take risks. I've done several programs on CNN on which I've been asked "Why do players, once they've been told they have a life-threatening condition, why do they continue to play?" My answer is always the same. "It's pride. It's pride in who they are, pride in being able to demonstrate the talent they have and it's pride in being a part of a team." I think back years ago and I think of athletes such as Jack Morris, who you might or might not know was a great pitcher with the Minnesota Twins in 1991 when the Braves played the Twins in the base-ball world series. Here was an older pitcher who no one expected to be able to pitch more than five innings in any game. Instead, in the deciding game, because of his pride in what he had done and the pride he had in what he was able to do for his team, he not only pitched a complete game, but he pitched a complete game plus extra innings to win a World Series game. You have to ask yourself, how could that happen? It happened because no matter how tired you get many times, you're always able to pull out a little more. There's always a little more left in the tank. I think of John Smoltz who in 1991 was young kid whose record was 2 wins and 11 losses the first half of the year and the second half of the year, he won 14 out of 16 starts. It was the biggest pitch-er turn-around since 1918. How did that happen? It happened because he had so much pride in himself and in his team and in his talent that he was able to pull out extra every game. The players behind him played better ever game than they did the first half. Why? Because they sensed he was pitching to win every time he took the mound. It was really fun to watch in '91. After that, John Smoltz became the record holder for the most post-season wins in baseball and held that record for many years. Again the reason was pride. We can't talk about that too much. I think too many times people lose their pride because of too much mud in the water, too many things on their mind. They are concerned about too many things over which they have no control. They forget to control the things that they can deal with. After so much adversity, they begin to lose their pride, pride in their job, and pride in their ability to be a father, to be a husband, to be a good friend. There's nothing more frustrating than to deal with someone who has lost the ability to feel good about themselves. If you are able to take this information and use it, one of the outcomes will be that you will have more pride in who you are. You will have more pride in your professional and personal endeavors. I think one of the outcomes also will be that when you begin to understand better why you do what you do, your balance will become much better, not in terms of quantity of time maybe, but in terms of quality time; time you spend with your family and time you spend at work. It is also critical that balance be one of your primary goals. Once you have that pride, you are able to experience the sweet taste of integrity. You will then know what motivates you. You will achieve and you will be able to be more persistent in your achievements.

Another area that is really not emphasized in programs, seminars and books, is the value of just looking around and learning. It may seem relatively simple and a lot of times we say we look around. But we don't learn. We observe, but we don't understand what we're watching. I guess everyone spends a lot of time thinking and wondering and thinking and wondering. Thinking about moving ahead and wondering what they would have done differently if given another chance. It's amazing that when we think and wonder, we look around, but we don't see anything. Consequently, we don't seem to learn anything. It's interesting to me how much money we spend on seminars to learn how to listen, how to learn and how to communicate. These are all things which would happen naturally if we would just give ourselves a chance. If you look at a couple of real life examples that were mentioned in a previous chapter, looking around can teach us about life and motivation and pride and managing. The two groups that I talk about often are obviously kids and old folks. If you go to a playground and watch kids play, they create things, they make rules, they play the game, they reach an outcome, they go home. Creativity is probably the operative term to talk about here. In order to get the mud out of the water, in order to be productive, to set goals, to organize a plan, in order to put the right team in place and select the right coach to help you move ahead, you also have to be creative. Everybody is as creative now as they were when they were children. For some reason, as we become adults, we put our creativity talents on the shelf. I ask groups in seminars how many people are as creative now as they were when they were kids. Nobody raises their hand.

But everyone is as creative as they were if they would only open up and let it out. Creativity may result in mistakes, it may entail risks, but creativity is such a critical factor in enabling you to move ahead with your life. If you're burdened with a disability or a chronic disease, something that has taken away many of your physical, and sometimes cognitive abilities, then essentially in order to move ahead with your life, you have to be creative. I have to be creative every day with MS. For example, when I've written some books, I've been able to sit down and write a chapter in one weekend. Since I've gotten MS, I'm not able to do that. I can't write for more than an hour before I have to put it away. I then have to go back later and reread what I've written because I can't remember what I've written. It's very frustrating at times, but it forces me to be creative in order to complete the project and make things happen. I think based on being around athletes and corporate people as much as I have in the last 39 to 40 years, creativity is nothing more than unused common sense. It seems the more mud we get in the water and the more frustrated we become, the first thing to go is common sense. When I talk about solutions to issues that my clients have, I see them look at me in a strange way sometimes and they're thinking, "Geez, that's just common sense." Well, certainly it is just common sense. But it seems to be the first thing we forget. Take a common sense approach to getting the mud out of the water. Take a common sense approach to dealing with people and putting your team in place and looking at your assets and liabilities. Common sense is such a wonderful trait that everybody has, but very few seem to use.

The other group that I've talked about in the text is the old folks. I don't know why we neglect old folks, why we put people out to pasture when they reach a pre-established age, usually around 60, unless we decide to make that 55. I confess to total ignorance regarding age discrimination, perhaps because I've turned 67 or because I've learned most of life's lessons from older people. One lesson that comes to mind, and I'm sure everyone who reads this text can recall similar experiences, is to have you think about some common sense things that have happened to you in your life and influenced our decisions. I had a grandfather who was a welder on the railroad for 45 years. His job was pretty well defined. Ride the the rails in a small vehicle and repair the rails which were chipped or rough for some reason. He lived much of that time in what were called camp cars, actually freight cars which had been converted to homes on rails. Trains would pull his camp car from city to city and park it on the sidetracks and he would work for a week and then go to another city. As a child, I remember spending lots of time living on those freight cars. Probably the best experiences I've ever had in my life, were when you were sleeping on a sidetrack at night, fast freight trains would come by and shake you right out of your bed. You got up the next morning, put everything back on the shelves and it was an adventure. The question is what would motivate a person to do this for 45 years? It's a life's lesson. It was pride. Pride in knowing the rail was better when he left it than when he started. Pride in knowing that rail travel was safer and pride in a job well done. We need to examine our environments and define why we do what we do and you may be tired of reading about why we do what we do, but nothing is more important in life than to understand your purpose. When preparing for a convention speech recently, I inquired about the age range of the participants. I was delighted to learn that the range from 28 to 100 years old. An active member, a hundred years old, who works every day. Why? Because he wants to, because he has pride in what he brings to the work environment every day. Can you imagine the things that younger people learned from him? Not about business, marketing or technology, but how to live to be 100. I could write page after page of these examples, but I think my purpose here is to cause you to think about examples from your own life when you think back over the years about people who have been around you and from whom you were able to learn life's lessons. Hopefully, pride was one of them. Hopefully everyone will be able to feel that pride when you complete the tasks that have been presented to you in this text.

In summary, I want to talk about two examples that have had a tremendous influence on my life. Again, I mention these hopefully so that you can think of examples in your own life. I was speaking to an MS group in California a few years ago. After I spoke, I was signing books for the participants and a lady came up to me in a wheelchair. She said, "Thanks" and I responded, "I'm glad you liked it." Her response was, "You don't understand. I've been planning my suicide for three weeks and tonight you've opened my eyes and I'm going to be fine." At that moment, I looked at the World Series Championship ring on my hand and I thought, you know, this ring pales in comparison to what just happened here. Maybe for one of the first few times in my life, I really felt good about being able to help someone open their eyes. I really didn't open her eyes, obviously, she did it. But at least I gave her some things to think about in her life and she responded to those. This is an example I will never forget as long as I live.

The other example happened to me shortly after I was diagnosed with MS. I had made my living for 39 years working outdoors, working on baseball fields, tennis courts and golf courses. When I was diagnosed with MS, because of the problems with heat, I wasn't as able to do as many of those things anymore. I was going into the baseball stadium in Atlanta one night and I was walking up the steps. A homeless person approached me and he had a bag of aluminum cans on his back. He walked up to me and asked, "Are you Dr. Jack?" I said, "Yes, I am. What can I do for you?" He said "nothing for me." He said, "We live up here." He was pointing to a bridge. Apparently he and his buddies live under that bridge. He said, "My buddies and I read about your MS in the Atlanta Constitution. They sent me down here to tell you that we're praying for you, and we sure hope you get to feeling better." He turned and walked away. Even when I talk about this, I get emotional because it's incredible where things come from to help you. Any time you help other people, you don't need to look for help in return from those people because somebody somewhere is planning to do something for you. It was just an incredible event in my life. Any time I feel I've got too much mud in the water, the issues are overwhelming and there doesn't seem to be a light at the end of the tunnel, I think of that homeless man and the fact that he was more concerned about me than he was about himself. I think there is somebody somewhere who is that concerned about you. If you continue every day to get up in the morning with the intent and goal to help somebody, then you can rest assured that somebody somewhere is going to help you and they will touch your life. With this said, I hope you are now ready to make life-changing decisions and I hope you have enjoyed this conversation we've had. I hope you have a very fulfilling life and that you have a tremendous influence on others around you.

CONTACT INFORMATION

W^{**P**}

CENTER FOR WINNING PERFORMANCE
111 North Marietta Parkway, Unit A-217
Marietta, Georgia 30060

770-335-2885 • 770-426-5021 fax
centerforwinning.com
jlew18@AOL.com

*For information on Dr. Jack Llewellyn's availability for seminars,
speeches, and coaching, please contact Joe Pruss at:*

SERVING PUBLISHERS & AUTHORS
PASERVICES

PA SERVICES, LLC
Joe Pruss
4716 Buckskin Trail
Lilburn, Georgia 30047

770-564-1466 • 404-433-4291 mobile
pasllc@bellsouth.net

OTHER TITLES BY DR. JACK LLEWELLYN

Let 'em Play: What Parents, Coaches & Kids
Need to Know about Youth Baseball

ISBN: 978-1-56355264-8-0

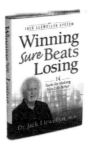

Winning Sure Beats Losing: 14 Tools for
Making Your Life Better

ISBN: 978-0-9844652-0-0

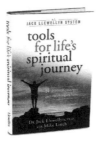

Tools for Life's Spiritual Journey: 14 Spiritual
Passages and Life-Changing Tools

with Mike Linch, Pastor

ISBN: 978-0-9844652-1-7

COMING SOON

Let 'em Cheer:
For Parents and Coaches of Competitive Cheerleaders

~

Winning vs Surviving Audio CD

~

Braking Traffic Stress Audio CD